Dr John Pearce is Emeritus Professor of Child Psychiatry at the University of Nottingham. He has written a wide range of practical books for parents as well as numerous articles for magazines and newspapers. He is a speaker at national and international conferences on childcare issues and is a member of numerous professional organisations and committees. He has worked with children and families as a child psychiatrist for over 25 years. John is married with three children.

Jane Bidder has been a journalist for the past twenty years and is a regular contributor to various national magazines and newspapers including *Woman, Woman & Home, The Times* and *The Daily Telegraph*. She is married to a solicitor and they have three children. As a result, they know all about sleepless nights! Jane represents the softly-softly approach in the book.

The New
Baby and Toddler
Sleep
Programme

How to have a peaceful night,
every *night*

Dr John Pearce

with Jane Bidder

VERMILION
London

For all sleepless parents

1 3 5 7 9 10 8 6 4 2

Text copyright © John Pearce and Jane Bidder 1997, 1999
Cover illustration © Nicola Smee 1997, 1999

First published in the United Kingdom in 1997 by Vermilion
This new edition published in the United Kingdom in 1999 by Vermilion
an imprint of Ebury Press
Random House, 20 Vauxhall Bridge Road, London SW1V 2SA

Random House Australia (Pty) Limited
20 Alfred Street, Milsons Point, Sydney, New South Wales 2061, Australia

Random House New Zealand Limited
18 Poland Road, Glenfield, Auckland 10, New Zealand

Random House South Africa (Pty) Limited
Endulini, 5A Jubilee Road, Parktown 2193, South Africa

The Random House Group Limited Reg. No. 954009

www.randomhouse.co.uk

A CIP catalogue record for this book is available in the British Library

ISBN 0 09 182591 1

Papers used by Vermilion are natural, recyclable products made from wood
grown in sustainable forests.

Printed and bound by Biddles of Guildford

Contents

Introduction

Pick up a selection of New Baby greetings cards and you're bound to find at least one with a cartoon picture of a typical New Father.

He'll be standing in a candlewick dressing-gown with heavy, half-closed eyes ringed with exhaustion. In the background, a baby will be screaming and – to drive the point even further home – the clock will be pointing to 3 a.m.!

We laugh because, as parents, we know it's not far from the truth.

New parents don't usually get much sleep. Suddenly, they are thrown from a normal civilised adult life into a semi-comatose existence centred around a small baby who sleeps fitfully when they least want him to. (Please note that unless a specific child is being written about, throughout this book your baby is referred to as a 'he', not because of any bias but to differentiate the mother or child carer from the baby.)

As that baby grows up, life doesn't always get much better. 'Does your child sleep through the night yet?' is a much-discussed question and topic of conversation from six weeks to five years – and even beyond. 'Does he come into your bed in the night?' is another question frequently asked by mothers.

Some babies *do* sleep regularly at night. Sometimes this is a matter of luck. But it also happens because their parents have worked at it. Yes, you *can* work on sleep just as you work at getting solids into that small reluctant mouth. Or persuading your toddler that he *can* be dry at night.

Sleeping is one of many habits which, as parents, we need to cultivate in our children. If you see it this way, it somehow becomes a more achievable goal. Instead of relying on luck, you can train your child – and yourself – into having unbroken nights.

Habits established during childhood tend to last into adult life, so it is important to try to set up good habits early on. This takes time, perseverance and repetition but is worth it in the end. Of course, children vary in how responsive they are to training at different stages of development. The developmental stages of sleeping and waking habits are explained in this book. If no specific age is mentioned, you can assume that the information applies to all children over the age of six months.

But it will probably take time. And you may feel you haven't got much of that at the moment.

If you persevere, you'll find there's a big pay-off at the end. Not only will you get that rest which you so badly need, you will also make sure that your child gets rest too. And he'll have learned yet another lesson in his long climb towards independence.

There's another plus, too. If you can get your child into a regular sleeping pattern, the whole family will benefit. Not just you but also your partner. Remember? The one who got you into this in the first place! It will also help any other children you have who need your attention, too. New babies often make siblings jealous. And it's no wonder if they are constantly awake and hogging the limelight.

So much for theory. What about the practice? How can we actually make that screaming baby or toddler go to bed?

Read on and see.

CHAPTER ONE

And so to sleep...

Everyone needs sleep. Not just children but parents too! It's amazing how much better we feel when we've had a good rest. Somehow, it's easier to deal with a difficult baby or child when we feel well inside ourselves. And sleep contributes to 'feeling well'.

Although we *know* that we need sleep, how can that help us to cope with a baby who wakes every half hour or a toddler who has decided that it's time to get up at 2 a.m.?

We tell ourselves that we need sleep and that our child can be taught how to stay happily in his bed. We persevere and hold on to a conviction that we *can* succeed.

· *Everyone is different* ·

Sleep can't be turned on or off at will but it *is* a habit and is one of the first routines which children need to get into.

However, about one in three children aged under five are reported to have disturbed sleep. And of these, 30 per cent could be said to have a serious problem.

· *Jeremy* ·

Jeremy was nine months old. He was the second child and his parents were astonished by how different he was from the first-born. Jeremy seemed to cry a lot but it was not ordinary crying: he would scream, go red in the face and his little body would go stiff with anger as he yelled. He was difficult to feed, difficult to settle, wriggly and certainly not cuddlesome. His mother began to believe that she must be doing something wrong or that perhaps she had been given the wrong baby by the hospital. She consulted

*the health visitor and the GP but nothing could be found wrong
with Jeremy. Then Jeremy's mother read in a magazine that some
children are born with a difficult temperament and they behave
just like Jeremy. She was pleased to read that most children with
a difficult temperament gradually settle down. The article
suggested that children like Jeremy benefit from a great deal of
routine in their life with very clear limits being set for their
difficult behaviour. At the same time they require extra loving
care and close supervision. Jeremy's parents put this into practice
and very gradually their persistence paid off and a year later
everybody remarked at how much easier Jeremy seemed to be. The
bedtime routine seemed to have been particularly helpful and
meant that the evenings had become a peaceful time for everyone.*

The good news is that as children grow older, their sleep
improves. By the age of eight, only one in 10 has sleep
problems. But eight years is a long time to wait until your
child gets a good night's sleep! Unless of course, you do
something about it . . .

· *What goes wrong?* ·

Why don't more children learn to sleep regularly and
consistently?

- Many families don't have a regular bedtime routine. Just
  as you needed a ruler to measure your child's window for
  bedroom curtains, so you need a yardstick to help you to
  decide when, where and how your baby/toddler/older
  child should go to sleep.

- Some children are better or worse sleepers than others. Those
  with strong emotions and irregular habits, for example, often
  find it hard to sleep without help. So do babies who had birth
  difficulties/babies with colic/children who are fed at night
  after one year/children over six months who sleep in the
  same room as the parents/children whose parents are over-
  worried or anxious.

- If we are over-tired, we will probably find it difficult to be firm and consistent. It's understandable, after all. When we're under stress, we all do things we wouldn't do if we were feeling more relaxed.

- Parents easily feel guilty, which can lead to over-compensation. You've been at work all day. So why can't your child stay up a little later than usual? You've told off your child for something during the afternoon. He's upset. If he stayed up for a little later, it would give you time to 'make up'.

- Confusion. Your doctor, health visitor, mother-in-law, mother and friends have all given you advice. Each piece of advice is different! What on earth should you do?

· *Why do anything?* ·

Why not leave your child to sleep when he wants to? He'll sleep when he wants to, won't he? Yes, but . . .

- Will it fit in when *you* want him to sleep? If your child isn't sleeping in a way which fits in with your way of life, everyone is going to feel upset and irritable.

- Lack of sleep in children and adults leads to poor concentration and irritability.

- When adults get tired, they tend to slow down. But when children get tired, they often speed up and become hyperactive – not a good combination!

- A tired and irritable child is not easy to deal with. And if *you* haven't had much sleep yourself, it won't make for a very happy family . . .

- If you encourage your child to develop a good sleeping habit, it will actually bring you closer. Yes, really! You'll get to know what his limits are. You'll find out how tough he is and how he ticks. Through 'negotiating' a sleeping pattern – on your terms and not his – you'll be encouraging him to respect you as a parent. Some of this might sound rather old-fashioned and perhaps unfashionable, but you'll be surprised at how much respect and rest can help you both.

· *Help is at hand!* ·

The first step is to realise that every child and indeed every family is different. What might have worked for a friend or for your mother-in-law might not work for you. There are no right or wrong methods. But there *are* approaches which are better and more effective.

If you're a working mother, you might want to keep your child up during the evening to give you some extra time together. If that's the case, you also need to make sure that your baby/toddler's sleep needs are still being met.

On the other hand, you might prefer a traditional early-bed approach so you can rediscover the meaning of the word 'evening' and time for yourself!

The aim of this book is to help you to develop a plan tailor-made for your particular needs.

There are two ways of doing this: going in at the shallow end (known as 'gradual settling') or jumping in at the deep end ('rapid settling'). Nowadays, the accent on childcare has become very informal. 'Do what *you* feel is best' is the message from many parenting books and even health visitors and doctors. This can work for some parents but others need more definite guidelines, which is where a return to clear-cut, specific and firmer advice can help. In each of the following chapters, we'll be giving strategies for both the gradual approach (the shallow end) and the formal and stricter approach (the deep end).

The 'In at the deep end' approach

Imagine yourself going into a cold swimming pool, cold bath or a cold shower. As you shiver on the edge thinking about whether you should go in slowly or quickly you will probably feel quite uncomfortable. But with experience most people find that it is best to get in quickly.

Going in at the deep end requires confidence. But the uncomfortable bit is over and done with in a short period.

If you stay shivering on the edge you may never get in at all, which won't do your confidence any good. The problem of going in at the shallow end is that the discomfort is more prolonged and many people get half way in and decide to get out again.

Although generally it is best to get in quickly and go in at the deep end, this does not suit everyone. Some people much prefer to take things gradually and slowly, making progress little by little. We encourage you to take the rapid approach, but if you prefer to do things more gradually that is also OK.

Some parents might find the deep end a little tough to begin with. But the advantage is that you'll achieve faster results, especially if you begin early when your child is still a baby. The old motto 'Start as you mean to go on' makes sense. The shallow-end approach can be particularly useful for a child who has already developed bad sleeping habits and needs to be coaxed into a bedtime routine.

· *Bedtime means more than* · *going to sleep*

Going to bed means a lot more than simply going to sleep. It also means a time to rest. And it's a chance for your child's body to stop moving so fast and to recharge its batteries.

The best proof is to watch your child when he's in that lovely relaxed state, just before drifting off to sleep or just after waking up. Who knows what is going on inside your baby/toddler's mind when you catch him lying awake in his pram/crib/cot, gurgling to himself or staring at the mobile above him. Whatever it is, it's important to *him*. He's resting in bed and learning to enjoy it at the same time. It's a habit you should be encouraging.

At bedtime, it's easy to forget the importance of resting the body. We often get very worked up about sleep. Because we feel so much better ourselves when we've had enough sleep, it's natural to get emotional when we *don't* have enough or think our children haven't had enough sleep. 'Why isn't my child sleeping? What is wrong with him – or us?' In fact, resting in bed is almost as good for you as sleeping. Resting in bed is something that parents can control even though no one can make a child sleep.

It might help to see sleep as the first habit or stage in your child's growing and learning process. Picture it as the first rung of a ladder. You're there to help your baby or child on to the bar. Once he's got there, he'll soon want to climb higher and higher.

Don't panic. Many parents understandably worry that their child will fall ill if he doesn't have enough sleep. In fact, nature is too clever for that to happen: instead, your child's body will automatically send him to sleep when he needs it. The problem is that this might not be at a time when *you* need it! Just look at all those toddlers who slump off in the back of the car during the afternoon school run to collect older children – and are then wide awake at 10 p.m. when their exhausted parents want to go to bed . . .

· *Growing up* ·

It also helps to remember that sleep is another stage in helping your child to be self-reliant. If you can catch your child early enough, it's quite possible to teach him not to be scared of the dark and actually to enjoy lying in his bed in the dark, even if he hasn't got his eyes closed.

Did you know?

Recent research suggests that babies and young children who sleep with the light on at night are more likely to be short-sighted than those who sleep in the dark.

Part of growing up is learning to be independent and feeling confident when alone. If your child is able to learn how to be alone in bed at night in the dark, this will help him to be confident during the day and to be more self-reliant.

Try to see a good sleep habit as an essential part of that 'helping your child to grow' process. If you do this, it becomes easier to dilute the emotion. Instead of feeling guilty about putting your child to bed because *you* need time alone, remember that you're doing him a favour, too. You're helping him to learn to enjoy his own company. And you're enabling him to grow physically and mentally because a child needs sleep as much as food.

· *Safe and sound* ·

All parents worry about whether their children are safe or not. And this is just as important when they're tucked up in bed. Bedrooms must be safe places (hence the phrase 'safely tucked up in bed'), but unfortunately, this isn't always the case.

Before putting your child to bed, you need to make sure he is safe:

- In the cot
- In the bed
- In the bedroom

- On the landing, down the stairs or anywhere else in the house where he is likely to wander during the night.

Ask yourself:

- Can he climb over the side of the cot?
- Can he get out of the window?
- If he wakes before you in the morning, can he help himself to anything dangerous in the kitchen or bathroom?

We'll be covering these points in greater depth within the following sections – but do remember that it's dangerous for you to be asleep while your child is on the loose.

· *Time for yourself* ·

Getting your child to bed is also crucial for you as a couple or, if you're on your own, for yourself as a person. Everyone needs time alone just as much as they need sleep. It's a time to unwind and become a grown-up adult once more instead of a parent who's busy keeping everyone else happy.

You also need space and time to communicate and be together with your partner and/or friends. It's easy to forget this. Your new baby is understandably the hub of your life. And it almost seems selfish to think about yourself or what *you'd* like to do on Saturday night.

But your baby will grow up eventually and make his own friends. He'll go to school, leave home and have babies himself. Where will you be by then? It might be too late to rediscover your friends or even your partner. But, if you've permitted yourself to have 'me' time from the beginning, you'll be able to have the best of both worlds. You'll have hung on to time for yourself, and you'll have created a self-reliant, happy child.

Again, we'll be showing you how you can achieve this.

· *How does everyone else cope?* ·

Before you choose which way is best for you, it's worth knowing how various cultures cope with sleep – or lack of it. If other countries do it differently, why shouldn't you? After all, most children eventually grow up into normal adults who will then, in their turn, worry about getting *their* children to sleep!

Italian and Spanish children, for example, frequently have midday siestas like their parents and then stay up late. About 50 per cent of African children co-sleep with their parents. Some say this helps them to become confident because they are never alone. Others argue that it delays the self-dependence process.

Japanese babies often sleep in the parental bedroom until they are toddlers. If you choose to do the same, the advantages are that you are more likely to hear your baby if he's sick or upset. But one big disadvantage is that your baby might well find it difficult to sleep alone when he's older.

Another problem is that you are both less likely to sleep well without waking during the night. One of you is bound to disturb the other either through turning over or talking in your sleep!

The Japanese often share beds with their young children, as indeed do 15 per cent of British families. Some will argue that this can be dangerous in case you squash your child and that he'll be less likely to accept his own bedroom when he's older. Others argue that it's a vital comforter.

The drawback is that you could become rather like a dummy for your child: he needs your presence as a constant reassurance.

If you share a bed with someone, you also quickly pick up any unsettled or distressed emotions. While it might be useful for you to know what your child is feeling, how much do you want your child to know when *you* are upset or unsettled?

Again, only you can tell which method is right for you. Each one has advantages and disadvantages which will be discussed in later chapters.

· *What is normal?* ·

Your friend's baby has been sleeping through the night since he was two weeks old, so what's wrong with yours? The answer is simple. Nothing. There's nothing like statistics to drain your confidence as a parent. But it's natural to want to know what the rest of the world is doing.

Officially, 70 per cent of babies are said to sleep from midnight to 5 a.m. by the age of three months. This figure rises to 85 per cent by the age of six months. But don't panic if yours is the only bedroom light on in your street at 2 a.m. Between the ages of 18 months and two years, half of those babies who had previously slept through the night suddenly start waking. So maybe life is fair after all!

This is also the time when children start resisting bedtime and resent being separated from their parents. It's not surprising really. How would *you* feel if someone pushed you out of the marital bed and said, 'Right, now you're on your own'? The trick, as the following chapters will show you, is to help your child, with the aid of routines and comforters, to enjoy being on his own, just as you are enjoying your independence downstairs in the sitting room.

Even when your child does finally fall asleep, he's quite likely to wake – even though that doesn't necessarily mean he'll get out of bed. So don't immediately go rushing up to his bedroom if you hear a slight rustling on the baby monitor. At the age of two months, for example, babies spend about 10 per cent of the night awake and about six per cent of the night awake when they reach nine months. But parents are only aware of this wakefulness if they make frequent checks or sleep with the baby.

· *Martin* ·

Martin was one month old and since birth seemed to have cried most of the time that he was awake. He cried before feeds and after feeds. During the daytime and during the night. His parents were in their early twenties and Martin was their first child. They were particularly worried because Martin only seemed to sleep for short periods during the day and cried for a long time during the night. Eventually, they took Martin to the paediatrician, who was unable to find anything wrong with him. The doctor explained that some children cry much more than others and that the normal sleep-waking cycle in the early days after birth is 20 to 30 minutes. The parents were reassured and found that if they made quiet shushing sounds, wrapped him up firmly in a blanket or rocked him gently, Martin quietened down quite quickly. They also found that if they left him to cry for gradually longer periods before going to him, Martin was much more likely to quieten himself down.

Research also shows that after six months babies take longer to go off to sleep – especially into a deep sleep. But the good news is that at six months many babies wake once or even twice during the night and still manage to go back to sleep without help. It makes sense, really, doesn't it? You – and probably your partner – turn over in the night and maybe open your eyes for a few seconds. But that doesn't mean you need someone to come rushing up to you with a cup of early-morning tea.

The six-month milestone is an important stage of development. This is when babies usually get into a clear daytime-awake and night-time-asleep rhythm. It is also the time when they start to see themselves as individuals and show anxiety when separated from a parent.

As children grow older, the pattern of their sleep continues to change. Newborn babies have phases of deep and light sleep which alternate in cycles of about 20 minutes. That's why it's easier to wake up your baby with a slight noise one day even though he didn't stir when you switched on the vacuum cleaner the day before. It's also why they often fall off to sleep during a feed – it doesn't mean they're not enjoying the milk!

These deep/light cycles become steadily longer until by the time your child is five or six, they occur every hour or so. When your child becomes an adult, these cycles will last between two to three hours, which is why you might find yourself waking up most often between 1 and 2 a.m. and 4 and 5 a.m.

· *Forging a habit* ·

During the first six months, your baby is still getting used to the new world in which he's found himself. A brand-new baby spends most of the day and night asleep but this isn't as good as it sounds because he'll usually only sleep deeply for 20-minute bursts. Just enough time for you to put the washing machine on again . . . If you are lucky, he will quickly learn how to doze off again after a short period of light sleep or waking.

By three months, children spend more time awake during the day than the night but will still wake four or five times during the night. They might stay quiet or they could try out those new lungs of theirs!

· *Jennifer* ·

Jennifer was three months old and had developed the habit of crying in the evening. Her parents found this particularly distressing because they both felt tired and they wondered if Jennifer actually knew that this was a time when they would do almost anything to keep her quiet. The health visitor explained that it is quite normal for babies between one month and three months to cry more in the evening than at any other time. They were also reassured to hear that most babies cry less and less after the age of three months and that excessive crying before that age does not predict crying at a later stage. It was less comforting when the parents heard that crying at night tends to increase between the age of nine months and a year and that even if they got Jennifer into a good night-time sleeping pattern it was quite likely that she would go through a phase of unsettled sleeping between the ages of two and three. This information made Jennifer's parents even more determined to get her into a good sleep routine at an early stage.

By about six months, however, there's light at the end of the tunnel. Most children will be sleeping through the night. And this is where you need to put your sleeping plan into operation.

If you leave it too late, the job will be much harder. The stable waking/sleeping cycle, which most six-month-old children begin to develop, will probably break down by two years if you haven't established a regular sleeping routine.

Just like toilet-training, feeding and dressing, sleeping is part of the daily routine. It is a habit and good habits don't always develop naturally; they have to be created by regular training and routine. And guess who's the trainer!

Forging a habit – and especially a sleeping habit – might be hard work. But when you achieve it, life becomes a lot easier. Think of it like learning to use a typewriter. At first, the letters seem all over the place, but then you learn the right keys in the right order. Eventually, through practice, you get a good result. It's the same with sleep training.

In the rest of the book, we will be dealing with the six major sleeping stages: getting your child to bed; staying in bed; going to sleep; staying asleep; sleep disorders, such as nightmares; and sleep behaviour, such as wetting the bed. Under each, we will suggest a variety of methods – it's up to you to try them out to see which hits the magic mark for you.

Sometimes, you'll want to 'pick and mix': a 'rapid settling' idea in one section might appeal to you and a more gradual approach from another might also do the trick. There are no hard and fast rules in this business as your baby knows all too well! But some 'tricks' will work better for you than others.

Remember, too, that putting your child to bed and getting him up in the morning is a good way of learning about him. You'll discover what works well and what he doesn't like. You'll find out how he reacts to pressure or how he behaves when things don't go his way. You'll see how independent and capable he is. You will also find out more about yourself and how you cope with your child.

How well, after all, *do* you know your little one? Can you tell when he is genuinely upset or when he is simply angry because he can't have you to himself all the time? How easily can he control you? Are you training him or is he training you?

· *Getting to know your child* ·

Each new baby arrives with its own special character. Some are remarkably easy to bring up, while others can be difficult to manage from the start, and it is a puzzle to work out what makes them 'tick'. It is not at all unusual for parents to feel that their baby is a stranger, visiting from another world. It takes time to get to know each other.

Training your child to have a good sleep routine will help you to get to know each other; however, it is better to know your child well before starting a sleep programme.

Parents naturally look at their new-born baby and try to work out what is going on in his little head: 'Oh look, she's smiling. She thinks you're really funny.' 'Now she's crying; you must have upset her.' It is easy to imagine all sorts of things that a baby might be thinking. Most of the time parents are probably quite wrong about what is going on, because we all tend to imagine that babies think like we do. Nobody knows for sure, but it is probable that babies' thoughts are rather like our experience of dreams, where time and logic are far from the real world as we know it.

You have to be careful about assuming you know what is

going on in your baby's mind. Beware if you hear yourself saying anything like the following:

'He doesn't want to go to sleep.'

'She's crying because she's frightened.'

'He must be hungry – even though he's just had a feed.'

'She's doing it deliberately to upset me.'

You may be right, but when your baby is young you will often be wrong about what he is communicating. This is why you need to get to know your child as quickly as possible.

Getting to know a baby is not much different from getting acquainted with a new friend. You need to spend time together with as little to distract you as possible. Look at your baby and talk. Tell him what you think about him and what you would like to happen now and in the future. Just keep on talking and observing – especially when he is crying. Try to talk in an everyday manner – as if you were discussing the weather – with as little expression of emotion as possible. Remember, crying is a baby's main way of communicating. It does not have the same significance as when an adult cries. Try holding your baby so that you are facing each other about 30 cm apart. Newborn babies focus best at this distance. Study the face closely and note how he reacts to you and to any change. Look particularly closely when he cries. How distressed is he really? Are there tears or does he soon stop crying if you distract him? Is this the time of day when he likes to have a crying session to air his lungs? Is he practising to become a pop star? You never know!

Don't expect to be able to 'read' your child for several months – and in some cases it may take years. Be patient and involve others so that you can find out what they think about your baby. It may be very different from your own interpretation.

· *Your personal chart* ·

Before you begin, you'll find it surprisingly useful to answer the sleep questionnaire on pages 25–7. This will help you to clarify what your child is *really* doing at night. For example, you might think your toddler is waking every night at 3 p.m. but if you make a note of it, you might find that it's actually five nights out of seven and that the time varies. If you can hit on a pattern, it's another clue to how a sleep problem can be solved.

- Did you know that breastfed babies wake more frequently than bottle-fed babies? The average age of sleeping through the night for a breastfed baby is 13 weeks compared with 11 weeks for bottle-fed babies. But there is no benefit in giving babies solid food to encourage sleeping through the night.
- Babies who cry during the night are more likely to have been put to bed asleep – instead of being put down and then allowed to go to sleep on their own.

That's really what this is all about: working out patterns and changing your behaviour accordingly. As the saying goes, 'You might not be able to change the dancer but if you alter your own steps, you can change the dance'.

· *Sleep questionnaire* ·

The purpose of this questionnaire is not to catch you out! It's simply to make you more aware of what you and your child are doing at night.

You might think, for instance, that you put your child to bed at roughly the same time each night; say, 7 p.m. But if you fill in this questionnaire every evening for a week, you might find that actually the time varies by as much as an hour.

As we explain later on, children's bodies are like ours. They have an internal alarm clock. When you go to bed an hour or two later than normal, you might not feel very rested. Nor will a child, even a young one. We quickly get into a routine of waking just before the alarm goes off in the morning. Children also rapidly develop waking habits – but not always at the time we would like them to.

When you've filled out the questionnaire, read it again. Give it to your partner to read. Ask yourself if there's anything you can learn from your answers. For example, does your child's late-afternoon nap stop him from resting when you put him to bed at 7 p.m.? Would it help if you brought his nap forwards into the early afternoon?

As you read through the book, refer back to the questionnaire. And add any extra comments you want at the bottom in the space provided. You will then be able to compare the advice in the book with what you are doing at present. Alternatively, you may prefer to copy the questionnaire onto a separate piece of paper.

1. How old is your child? _____

2. Is he in a crib, cot or bed? _____

3. How do you get him to sleep at the moment? Describe the routine. _____

   _____

   _____

4. How long before bedtime do you start this routine? ____

5. Is there a fixed bedtime? If so, what is it? _____

6. Where does your child sleep? _____

7. Does this location change during the evening. For example, does he start off in your bed until he is moved into his own? Or does he start off in his own and come

into your bed during the night? _____

_____

8. Does he share a bedroom with a parent or a brother/
    sister/someone else? _____

9. If you have other children, do they go to bed at the same
    time? _____

10. Will your child have had a nap during the day? If so, at
    what time and for how long? _____

11. Does he feel sleepy during the day but doesn't have a
    nap? _____

12. What kind of comforters does your child need to go to
    sleep with? (e.g., dummy/blanket/toy/you) _____

13. Is he scared of the dark? If so, are you? Do you leave a
    light on or the bedroom door open? _____

    _____

14. Will he stay in his cot/bed without trying to get out? Does
    he get out of bed during the night – where does he go?

    _____

15. Is he distressed when he's left alone in his cot/bed? If
    so, what do you do? _____

    _____

16. Does he headbang or rock his body? _____

17. Do you stay with him while he goes to sleep or do you
    leave him to go to sleep on his own? How long do you
    have to stay? _____

    _____

18. How long does it take him to go to sleep? _____

19. Will he rest quietly on his own before going to sleep? ____

20. Does he wake during the night? How many times? Is there a pattern? For example, does he wake at roughly the same times? _____

_____

21. What problems does he have in sleeping? When did they start and how often do they occur?_____

_____

22. Does he have nightmares? How often and at what time in the night? _____

23. Does he cry in the night? How often and for how long?

_____

24. Does he wet the bed in the night? Is there a pattern to this or an approximate time? How often? _____

_____

25. Does he sleepwalk? Is there any obvious reason for this? How often does he sleepwalk and at what time in the night?

_____

_____

26. Does he snore? _____

27. Does he fall out of bed? _____

28. What time (roughly) does he wake up?_____

29. Does he have to be woken? _____

30. What does he do then? (e.g., play; come into your bed; try and turn on the television)_____

_____

Other comments _____

_____

_____

_____

· *Parents' behaviour checklist* ·

Believe it or not, the way in which *you* behave can decide how well your child sleeps!

Just like the Sleep questionnaire, the Parents' behaviour checklist is not designed to catch you out. You don't score any marks – or lose any – at the end. But it *does* help you to think about what you're doing. And because of that, you may decide you could try doing certain things differently.

1. How much sleep do you get? Is it enough? Do you feel tired during the day/evening/both? _____

2. How many adults are involved in putting your child to bed? _____
   _____

3. Does your partner come home late? _____

4. Does his or her arrival disturb your child's sleep routine?
   _____

5. How do you react if your child cries in his cot/bed or tries to get out? _____

6. If you have other children, how do you look after them while you're getting the younger ones to bed? _____
   _____

7. Do you 'give up' if your child won't sleep and let him stay with you in the evening? _____

8. Are you consistent when you say 'yes' or 'no' to your child? _____
   _____

9. Do all the adults at home have the same ideas as you about your child's sleeping routine? _____

10. Does it make you argue? _____

11. If your partner thinks you should get your child down to bed in a different manner, have you let him or her try it out? _____

12. Does your child prefer you or your partner to put him to bed? _____

13. What would happen if one of you went out of the house and the 'less experienced' person had to do it? _____

_____

14. Does your child come into your bed at night? _____

15. Do you or your partner mind? _____

16. Does your child's night-time behaviour interfere with your sex life? _____

17. Do you 'check' your children when they're asleep? How often? _____

18. Does it disturb them? _____

19. What would happen if you didn't check them so regularly? _____

_____

20. How often do you wake up in the night? What do you do then? (e.g., turn over/lie awake/check the children/wake up your partner) _____

21. If your child wakes up early, do you take him back to bed/let him come into yours/get up and start the day early? _____

_____

22. Do you reward your older toddler/child if he's rested through the night and stayed in his own bed? If so, how? _____

23. Have you asked for professional help on your child's

sleeping habits? What was the most/least useful advice you'd pass on to another parent? _____

_____

24. If you were a new parent again, what would you do/not do when trying to get your child to sleep? _____

_____

25. Are you a relaxed parent or do you worry a lot? Are most of these worries unnecessary? Is there a particular reason for these concerns? (e.g., stillbirth/miscarriage/cot death/ depression/general anxiety/insecurity)

_____

26. What do you remember from your own childhood about sleeping and going to bed? Were you afraid of the dark? _____

27. Have you ever left someone else in charge – apart from your partner – to put your child to bed? What happened?

_____

28. If not, why not? Are you worried that your child won't let anyone else do the job? _____

_____

29. Is there general family stress which might affect your child? _____

30. Who, in the family, is affected by your child's inability to sleep well? _____

31. Have you got a way of making it clear to your child that you are really serious and mean what you say? _____

32. Can your child tell from your face that you are determined that he must do what you say? _____

_____

• CHAPTER TWO •

Safety and getting your child to bed

For your own peace of mind, you need to know that your child will be safe when you leave him at night. Just as you make sure he is safe during the day, so you should do the same when evening comes.

· *Safety* ·

How safe is your child's bedroom? If you're going to expect him to stay for a long period of time in his room alone, you must make sure that he can't harm himself in it. He must be totally safe.

Study the following checklist to make sure the room is child-proof. It's easy to get neurotic about safety and one of the best ways to deal with this understandable fear is to make sure that your child is as safe as possible.

- **Crib/cot**   Does it conform to British Standards or a similar European safety mark? Beware of old or second-hand items which might have loose parts which a child could swallow or toxic paint.
- **Mattress**   Does it fit snugly into the frame? If there's a gap, your child might become trapped.
- **Cot bumpers**   Could your child get caught up in these and pull on him if he tries to get out? If you're worried, remove them.
- **Bed**   If your child has just graduated to a bed, you may decide to a buy a bed guard (an extra, temporary 'side' to

prevent children from falling out of bed). Again, make sure they comply with current safety standards and that your child cannot get trapped.

Alternatively, place blankets or a duvet on the floor next to the bed so that if he falls out, he won't hurt himself.

- **Sleeping position**   Until your baby can turn over on his own, make sure he sleeps on his back and not his front.
- **Windows**   Can your child climb out of the window? Have you put window locks in place?
- **Heating**   Never leave an electric bar fire on or one which could catch fire if your child interfered with it. If you have an oil-filled plug-in radiator, make sure your child can't touch it or pull it over on top of himself.

  If you don't have central heating, make sure your child is dressed in warm layers according to the weather. Remember that, especially for young babies, it's just as dangerous to be over-warm as it is to be over-cold. Check by placing your hand against your baby/toddler's cheek. It should feel the same temperature as your own body.
- **Toys**   Supposing your child put the cord on a pull-along toy around his neck? Toys like this should have been put away before bedtime. Watch out too for balloons which could be swallowed if burst.
- **Furniture**   Is that wardrobe firmly in place or could your child pull it down on top of him? What about that chest of drawers or that chair which he might try to climb up on?
- **Door locks**   Can your child lock himself inside his room? If so, remove the lock.
- **Baby monitor**   A plug-in monitor will help you to hear if your child is in trouble. But use it with caution. Don't go running up every time you hear your child turning over. This will only encourage him to wake up and break the habit of sleeping!

  Rather than keeping the monitor on all the time – which can take control of your life as you listen out for every little sound – it would be better to turn it on briefly from time to time just to check that all is well and then turn it off again.

- **Electric sockets**   These should be covered with child-proof caps from Mothercare, etc.
- **Pillows**   Pillows can actually be dangerous for young babies because they can interfere with their breathing. As a general rule, wait until your toddler is between a year and 18 months old at the earliest. Young children don't need a pillow. When you *do* give your child a pillow, start with one that is both firm and thin.

How to check your baby is safe

It is absolutely essential for parents to know that their child is safe. Parents check their new born baby very frequently. As time passes you will be able to go for increasing periods without checking and you will learn to 'read' your child to know whether he is unwell or not.

The more frequently children are checked by their parents during the night the more likely they are to cry and be disturbed. Therefore every parent must find a way of knowing that their child is safe in bed with the minimum amount of interference. Here are some suggestions:

- A baby alarm which you switch on to check that your baby is breathing quietly and restfully and then switch it off again.

- The door cracked slightly open so that you can see your child in bed through the gap.

- A mirror or the reflection of the glass of a picture positioned on the wall so that you can see round the door without having to go into the room.

- A dimmer switch or a torch will avoid the need to switch on a bright light.

> • Bend over and look through the door so that your
>   head is not where your child would expect it to be
>   when the door opens or you could fit a peep-hole in
>   the door.

· *Getting your child to bed* ·

Getting your child to bed may sound like the easy part. But
the way in which you do it builds the cornerstone for the
whole foundation. If you do this in the right way for you
and your child, you'll be more likely to succeed in your
ultimate aim of getting a good night's rest and having a
happy child during the day.

Think of it from their point of view. Supposing you're
happily reading a book in the sitting room or watching a
favourite television programme. Suddenly, someone
yanks you by the collar, says, 'Right, time for bed' and
marches you straight to your bedroom. The chances are
that you won't feel calm or relaxed enough to rest, let
alone sleep. Children, like adults, need a wind-down
period to bridge that gap between an active day and a
quiet night.

As you have probably found out, a simple 'Go to bed!'
rarely works. An older child will pick up the vibes in your
desperation. Even a baby will sense your distress and, in
turn, feel unsettled.

Instead, hang on to a key word: ROUTINE. Picture it in
big letters over the bedroom door. And believe in it. Over
the past few years, routine has become an old-fashioned and
sometimes maligned term. But if you can get your children
into a good bedtime routine, you'll be surprised at the
difference it makes.

After all, you have your own internal clock, don't you? If
you're used to going to bed at 10 o'clock and you suddenly
have a week of getting there at 11 o'clock instead, you'll feel

tired and irritable. A child has his own internal clock, too. The only difference is that he's waiting for you to set it. If you don't do it soon, he'll set it himself to a time which doesn't fit in with your plans!

· *Young babies* ·

Young babies will still be finding their own routine, so the trick is to start putting them to bed when you sense they are about to drop off. Watch out for warning signs like droopy eyelids or that special tired cry which you'll be learning to recognise. Then head for the cot.

If he wakes as you put him down, try:

- Making loud shushing sounds.
- Humming.
- Gently stroking his head.
- Any sound that is repetitive and rather boring.

· *Gary* ·

Gary's mother had found it difficult to sleep since his birth five months previously. This was partly because he cried a lot during the night but over the last month or so, she had been waking very early in the morning even though he was sleeping quietly. She found herself feeling progressively more tired and miserable. She felt that she was not coping with Gary and that she was letting her husband down. Eventually she asked her GP for some sleeping pills for both herself and Gary. The GP diagnosed that Gary's mother had a puerperal depression, which usually responds very well to medical treatment and Gary's mother was soon feeling much better in herself. Unfortunately, Gary continued to wake frequently at night. It seemed as though he had got into a habit of waking. When he woke up he would normally cry until somebody came into him. His parents had tried everything to calm him down and stop the crying: they made him comfortable, gave him cuddles, rocked him quietly, sang lullabies and hummed, switched on various machines to make a constant humming sound, put a clock with a loud tick by him, carried him around in their arms, winded him, massaged him . . . Sometimes one thing would work and sometimes another. When they consulted their GP it was agreed that now that Gary's mother was feeling better in herself and there was no evidence there was anything wrong with Gary, he should be left to cry. Both parents felt that was too difficult, so they decided that they would leave him to cry for three minutes before going in and then delay the time of going in by one minute each day. This worked well. Gary started to get the message after a week and was into a good sleep routine three weeks later.

· *Older babies and toddlers* ·

When your child is six months old you could start the sort of routine which you would follow for older children, since even little ones learn to recognise signs such as dimming the lights and singing a lullaby.

Some of the other routine signs – such as tidying away toys – may not be relevant. But even a young toddler can help to fill up the toy box.

Start by getting your child ready for bed at the same time every evening. This isn't easy if you have other children who might need collecting from Brownies or friends. So aim for a reasonable time which will allow for all these eventualities.

The kind of routine you now follow will depend on you and your circumstances. But here are some examples in chronological order.

TIP: If this order doesn't suit you or you want to devise a different bedtime routine, that's fine. But the trick is to keep the same order every night. The repetition will calm and reassure even very young children.

TIP: Make sure you've tired your child out during the day. If he's had a brisk afternoon walk or play in the garden, he'll be more likely to be ready for bed.

· *Suggested bedtime routine* ·

- Allow a suitable period of time – at least half an hour – to let your child's tea go down before you start the run-down to bed.

- Always follow the same routine. Do everything in the same order with the same timing.

- Calm down excited games and switch off the television.

- Close the curtains and dim the lights.

- Encourage toddlers to tidy up toys as a 'winding-down' process.

- Run the bath and, if he's old enough, invite your child to get his towel and nightclothes ready. Is he used to having a drink of water by the side of his bed? If so, make sure it's in place. This way, he's less likely to run off while you're looking for missing items.

- Enjoy a fun bathtime but try to avoid rowdy games which will excite him and wake him up.

- Encourage an older child – two years upwards – to look at the clock. Use the clock in the sitting room to signal the start of the bedtime routine and a clock in the bedroom to signal the time to be in bed. A novelty design such as an animal whose eyes move as the clock ticks might appeal to your little one and make this exercise fun.

  Most children can't read the time properly until the age of seven or eight. But you could put a marker on the clock to show bedtime.

Help him to read the time and reinforce it. 'Yes, six o'clock. Bedtime.' This is a way of getting the clock to control your child. Instead of you being an ogre, the clock is deciding that it's time to turn out the light and go to sleep.

- Tuck up a favourite doll/toy into a doll's cot. Time for dolly's bed? Then it's time for your child to go to bed too.

- Tuck your child up in bed and read a story together. Say your prayers together, depending on your beliefs. Make sure he's got his special comforter (such as a cuddly toy) but make sure it's safe. (See the safety check list on pages 31–2.)

- Sing a soft lullaby. Even older children enjoy this, especially if you've always done it. It's a reassuring ritual like a well-known nursery rhyme. You don't have to be a great singer or even sing in tune for this to be calming. It's the familiar sound that has the effect.

- Say your special goodnight phrase. This might be simple, like 'Good night, sleep tight'. But always keep it the same. Children love ritual. They enjoy the same things over and over again, like a favourite story. And it makes them feel that all is well with the world.

- Keep the time you spend with your child when he is in bed fairly short. The longer you stay, the greater the protests when you leave – and the more crying there will be during the night.

- Turn out the room light, leave the landing light on if necessary. Then *go out of the room* and shut the door. Remember you have already made sure the room is safe and you can use the baby monitor to check that all is well.

Special 'magic' bedtime phrases

Use these when you put your child down to bed and again if he wakes up in the night. The familiar words will soothe him:

- NIGHTY, NIGHTY, SLEEPY TIGHTY
- GOOD NIGHT, LITTLE ONE
- SHHHH, SHUT YOUR EYES. GOODNIGHT
- SWEET DREAMS
- GOD BLESS, SLEEP WELL

· *Common questions* ·

Here are some common questions from parents about bedtime routine, together with answers on how to solve individual problems.

'Even the word "bedtime" upsets my toddler'

'I only have to mention the word "bedtime" and my toddler gets very upset. I can't cope with the outburst and all those tears. What can I do?'

Use the clock. It's not you who says it's bedtime. It's the clock. So there's nothing you can do about it. Don't make a big issue about bedtime either. Treat it as an immovable event like teatime. You need to eat. And you need to go to bed.

If your child is old enough, you could talk about other children going to bed and maybe animals, too. If it's dark, you could use that as an evidence that it's time to go to bed. But don't reason too much with your child. Or he might win the argument!

'My two-year-old uses delaying tactics!'

'When I say it's time for bed, my two-year-old – and her four-year-old sister – beg me for one more story or one more television programme. I feel mean saying "no". Should I stick to my guns?'

Definitely. Use that routine as your yardstick. Without it, you're lost! After all, when does 'one more' stop? It's like eating and crossing the road safely. Your child needs to learn that when you say 'no', you mean it. This isn't being hard. It's merely setting boundaries. Children actually like knowing how far they can go. It's another way of making them feel secure – even if they don't seem to appreciate it at the time!

· *Samantha* ·

Samantha, aged three, and her brother Josh, aged five, were not keen on going to bed. They were particularly good at delaying tactics. The favourite was 'just one more'. One more game, one more story, one more page, and so on. If this strategy did not work they had a number of trump cards up their sleeves. These included: 'I need to go to the toilet', 'I feel sick' and 'My tummy hurts'. Their father was a doctor and had to work long and irregular hours. The children never knew when their father was going to be at home and they were naturally keen to stay up and see him. Father thought this was a good idea but mother was not too sure because it always led to protests and refusal to go to bed. In fact, bedtime had become a nightmare. On the advice of father's colleague at work the parents decided to start a very regular bedtime routine taking it step by step in a predictable way, leading up to getting into bed and saying goodnight. Each stage was timed exactly by the clock. This meant that father was often not at home to see the children although he managed to change his on call duties so that he was more likely to be at home at bedtime. It wasn't long before the children were actually reminding their parents what the routine was. And instead of controlling their parents by thinking of ways of delaying bedtime, they started to insist that their parents keep to their side of the agreement to put them to bed at the right time and keep precisely to the routine. The parents were delighted because everything became so much easier in the evenings.

'Our family life is too complicated to have a routine'

'We have three children and there's so much going on that it's too difficult to have a set routine every evening. What should we do?'

Life is too complicated *not* to have a routine. You have a choice, of course, but you will probably find that without a set pattern, your evening becomes chaos. Perhaps you should try cutting down on all the different things you do at this time.

Sometimes, it's easy to do too many activities, even though you're only doing it for the children's 'good'. Maybe it's worth making some sacrifices to create a calmer evening. Once you've established a basic routine, you'll be able to make one or two exceptions for a one-off event.

'My daughter refuses to get out of the bath'

'My four-year-old daughter won't help me to help her to get ready for bed. She won't get out of the bath or brush her teeth. What should I do?'

Try making a game out of it – but one which is serious at the same time. Use counting. 'Let's count to ten and by then you should be out of the bath.' If that doesn't work, pull out the plug and tell her you'll put the cold tap on. Say this in a jokey way but make sure you carry out your 'threat'! For slightly older children – five upwards – try counting in French. The novelty might intrigue them enough to stir themselves.

Another 'game' is to start a running commentary ('Emily is getting out of her bath and she's cleaning her teeth') but make sure you say each phrase as she does the action. She'll probably start to join in the fun and it will make her want to go faster.

[See also the 'Unco-operative child' box on page 48]

'My son insists on having lots of teddies in his bed'

'My son insists on having lots of teddies in his bed. It's become ridiculous because there's hardly room for him. If I make a fuss, he won't go to bed. What should I do?'

You're right. There won't be enough room for him. He won't feel comfortable and that could upset his sleeping pattern. So suggest you find one or two 'special sleeping' teddies who are only there for bedtime. You could even find special 'toy nightdress' clothes for the teddies to make their bedtime more of an occasion, too.

'The door has to be left open'

'My two-year-old insists the door is full open. Is this wrong?'

A wide-open door gives the message that it's only safe outside. It suggests that life is so dangerous that Mummy or Daddy needs an open door so they can come rushing in at any time! Ideally, you need to start off with a shut door so children aren't taught to be scared of being alone.

But if they have already learned to be scared, you could try gradually closing it until there's a little gap or maybe none at all.

You could try making this into a game with older children by putting marks on the floor with the name of the day attached to them. On Monday, it will be so far open. On Tuesday, it will be closed a bit more. And so on.

'I have to lie down with him'

'My 18-month-old will only go to bed if I lie down with him. I haven't time to do this because we have a new baby as well. What can I do?'

Children *do* need comforting. It's natural. But are you going to be his comforter for the next five years? If you lie down with your child every time he goes to sleep, he's more likely to cry out for you when he wakes up. After all, he's dropped his dummy (in other words, you) and he needs you back.

See Chapter Four on Crying and the Three-Day Sleeping Plan.

If you really feel you have to stay with your son, try the gradual approach of sitting by his bed and then gradually reducing the amount of time.

· *Robert* ·

Robert was four and his father had left home a year previously. Naturally, Robert's mother was upset about what had happened and Robert missed his father. Neither he nor his mother had been sleeping well and they found they got a great deal of comfort from being together in the evening. Robert would eventually fall asleep at about 10 o' clock and his mother would carry him upstairs into her own bed. If she did not do this, he would wake screaming during the night. It seemed to work quite well but Robert tended to be restless during the night and he frequently woke his mum up. She went to the GP to get some night sedation either for herself or Robert or both. She didn't mind too much because she was becoming quite exhausted. The doctor told her that she should get Robert into a good sleep routine and move him into his own bedroom. The GP refused to prescribe any drugs for sleeping. In spite of all her efforts, Robert's mum was unable to get him into a routine of going to bed. He was so difficult and demanding and she felt that it was cruel to force him to do something that made him upset, particularly after his father's departure. Eventually she went back to the GP to ask for some sleeping pills. The GP explained that although medication can help people to sleep over a short crisis period, it would in the end make it more difficult to sleep properly and it was very easy to get hooked. The GP suggested that Robert's mother should not be too concerned about what was happening at home and if she found it easier to carry him upstairs asleep and put him into her bed then that was fair enough. However, she should realise that this would make Robert more likely to wake during the night and that if they continued to sleep together it would be easy for Robert to pick up his mother's distress and that this could interfere even more with his sleeping. When she was ready to get Robert into a good bedtime routine she should contact the health visitor. The problems continued, and two months later Robert's mother decided that she would have to get Robert into a better sleep habit and put him to bed in his own room. She didn't contact the health visitor but got the support of her mother and several friends who lived nearby. They all worked together to help Robert's mum keep to the plan. One idea that proved particularly helpful was to have an alarm clock that went off at the time that they had fixed for

Robert to be in bed. If the bedtime routine was getting behind schedule, Robert would look at the clock and suddenly speed up, leaping into bed just before the alarm went off.

'What can I do when the clocks change?'

'My children won't go to sleep when the clocks change in summer and winter. In summer, they say it's too light. And in winter, they aren't tired when it's bedtime.'

It's a good excuse, isn't it? But adults do it. Even animals. Your dog may not be used to going to bed at 9 p.m. when it was 10 p.m. last night. But he does it. So do children all over Europe. And so can yours. Try:

- Buying a curtain liner to make the bedroom curtains thicker in the summer. That way, the light won't come in so much.

- Using the clock. It may feel like 6 o'clock. But the clock says 7 o'clock. So it *is* bedtime.

'What should we do in the holidays?'

'We find it difficult to get our under-fives to sleep on holiday when the routine is disrupted. We have the same problem at weekends, especially if we get back late from a day out. What should we do?'

It's best to stick to that routine wherever you are. But you can modify it slightly. If you want to go out to eat in the evening at a holiday restaurant, do so earlier. That way, you'll still be back around your child's bedtime.

It might sound restricting but it's worth hanging onto a pattern which you have tried so hard to create. Obviously, it's difficult to keep exactly the same routine on holiday. But you can retain certain key items like the goodnight phrase and the general bathtime run-down.

The same applies when you have visitors to stay at home. Although it might be tempting to keep your children up to see them, it could hurt a routine which is still quite new. When your routine is more firmly established, you can afford to do something different for the odd evening.

'What do I do with my other children?'

'I have other children to get to bed, too. How can I manage to include them all in the routine?'

Most parents discover that when you have one child, you wonder how you'll cope. But when you have two children, you realise how easy it was when you had just one! By the time some parents get on to number three or more, they often give up on bedtime. It's too complicated!

In fact, this is a mistake – not just for them but also for the older children. They need time alone with you, too. And graded bedtimes are also a good way of helping each child to feel different and special.

If you have two children or more, you can still stick to the earlier suggested routine. But stagger the times. Start off with the youngest and then, while he's resting in bed (if he's not, see Chapter 3: Keeping your child in his cot or bed), deal with child number two.

Alternatively, you might find it more practical to start the bedtime routine with all the children together and then put the older ones into their beds with a book while you sort out the youngest. When you've done that, you can move on to story time with number two and then number three. Provided, that is, that you've got any voice left . . . !

It helps to treat children differently because the more you treat them the same, the more jealous they are likely to be. If you were to try and spend exactly the same time with each child at bedtime, they would soon be counting the seconds and noticing any slight difference. Privileges like time for bed or lights out should be graded by ages so that the eldest has the 'best' deal.

This will help the eldest not to feel so jealous. The eldest is the only child who knows what it is like to have individual parental care and attention.

If the younger ones complain about their earlier bedtime,

remind them that they are moving up the ladder. This time next year they'll be able to stay up 15 minutes later, too!

Remember, too, that when you have got your children into bed, it is best not to spend too long with each of them. The longer you spend, the more wakeful your child is likely to be. After all, would *you* want to go to sleep if someone interesting was sitting at the end of your bed, having a good chat with you?

'My husband spoils my routine'

'My husband comes home just when I'm getting our baby and toddler to bed. He wants to see them but I want to get on with what we're doing. Am I being unfair?'

It's not easy, is it? It's natural for your partner to want to see his children after a day at work. You, on the other hand, have probably seen enough of them! Bedtime is often a matter of easing the parents into a routine as much as the child.

Sit down with your husband and work out what is best for you. If your husband really wants to see the children but simply can't get back earlier, help him to understand that he's not doing the children a favour by keeping them up. Suggest that he has them on his own for an hour or so at the weekend. Or perhaps he could change his work times. Is it really necessary to work late? How about starting earlier and finishing earlier?

If this causes problems, try it the other way round. Leave the children with your partner for the day (at the weekend again) and come back just as he is getting them down to bed. The partner-at-home will probably find it's not much fun . . .

Don't feel guilty either about your child not seeing both Mummy and Daddy at the end of the day. In an ideal world, it would be nice if he saw both of you. But it doesn't work like that when so many wage-earning partners commute. Instead, try:

- Ringing your partner after tea so your toddler can say goodnight.

- Encourage your toddler to draw a special picture for Daddy or Mummy which you can give to your partner when he/she returns.

- Give your partner a full account of what happened during the day. It is important for both parents to know what went on and for the child to know that his parents communicate about him. This will help him to feel loved and supported.

· *The routine isn't working* ·

If you've tried to establish a bedtime routine but it still isn't working, think about why it's not succeeding. Is it because:

- The adults in the house don't agree on bedtime rules? If so, sit down and work out a plan which you both favour. Children are very good at knowing if one parent is 'softer' than the other. Agree to agree. And remember, united we stand!

- You've got a difficult child. Some children *are* more difficult than others – just like adults. The three main characteristics of difficult children are:

  1. Very strong emotions.
  2. Unpredictable behaviour.
  3. Adapting to change slowly.

It helps to know you have a difficult child because then you understand it is not you!

The answer is to do more of the same. In other words, keep going with the routine, but:

- o Be more loving.
- o Be just as kind but firm, e.g., 'Yes, we'll tidy up those toys *now*.'
- o Make that routine longer and more involved. This will make your child feel secure. He knows what's coming next.

· *Anna* ·

Anna's parents found it difficult to agree about her bedtime routine. Her father was a bit like a sergeant major at home and expected everything to be done in the right order at the right time. He tended to shout if things didn't go according to plan. Anna's mother was an easy-going person and enjoyed changing the routine. If Anna wanted to stay up late, or if she was being difficult about the bedtime routine, her parents would almost always end up arguing. They tried not to do this in front of Anna but they found it difficult. Arguing usually led to Anna's older brother joining in and soon everyone in the family was upset. Eventually, the parents called in the health visitor and asked her to arbitrate between them. The parents were told that Anna would benefit from having a regular bedtime routine and once it was established it would then be possible to have the occasional change, because she would soon slip back into the routine again. The parents tried this and it seemed to be working well but they found that they still had disagreements. In the end it was decided that because Anna's father felt the more strongly about it, he should take over the bedtime routine.

How to cope with the unco-operative child

You've tried to start a bedtime routine but your child isn't keen to play ball! He won't turn off the television. He won't tidy away his toys. He winds up other children and pets. And he won't go to the lavatory.

Take a deep breath to calm yourself down and try out the following measures.

- **Won't turn off the television**? Take out the plug or remove the fuse. Tell your child you won't put it on the next day unless he allows you to turn it off. Then encourage *him* to do the switching off. Giving him a 'job' like this will make him feel more of a team.

- **Won't tidy toys away**? Tomorrow evening don't put out so many. Or make a game of it: 'You collect all the blue shapes and I'll find the red ones. Who can find the most?'

- **Winds up other children/pets**? Divide and rule. In other words, separate them. Distract an older child with a puzzle while you get the younger one ready for bed. Put pets in another room.

- **Won't go to the lavatory or get into the bath**? Try the 'running commentary' technique, e.g., 'Emily is going upstairs. She's making her way to the toilet', etc.
  Or, if you're feeling in the mood, think up a limerick:

> There once was a girl called Tink
> Who liked to bathe in a sink.
> One day she fell out
> And gave a great shout.
> 'Look Mummy, I've gone all pink!'

I know: it's silly, isn't it? But it will make you both laugh. That way, it reduces the tension, and your child will be more likely to do what you want.

- **Won't undress**? Try the counting method coupled with a challenge. 'See if you can get your jumper off by the time I count to five. Now see if you can take off your vest by the time I get to four.'
  Or the running commentary. 'Emily is taking off her jumper and now she's down to her vest . . .'
  Or, if your child is four plus, try helping her to name each part of her clothing in French, e.g., jupe for skirt. Even though they probably won't know the right answer, it's a distraction technique which will ease them into a routine. The following night, you can see if they can remember those strange French words.

· *Bedtime* ·

What time *is* bedtime? It's one of the ironies in parenting that many an exhausted adult's idea of a good evening is to go to bed early. But a child's ideal evening is to go to bed as late as possible.

When they get older, this becomes a competition. 'My friends' parents let her stay up until such and such a time. So why can't I?'

Even though your child is too young to swap bedtime notes with friends, it won't be long before he does! So be firm about bedtime from the word go and it will help you in the long run.

Setting a definite time for your child is a good way of helping you both to achieve independence. You need the time for yourself and for your partner. A child will also learn to respect boundaries if he knows that when the long hand reaches twelve and the short hand reaches eight, it's time for bed.

You can also use bedtimes to make him feel grown up. If an eight-year-old knows he goes to bed 20 minutes later than his six-year-old sister, he'll feel responsible and will be more likely to act accordingly.

The actual time depends very much on your lifestyle. If you have to pick up your eight-year-old from Cubs at 7 o'clock on Tuesday evenings, it wouldn't be very sensible to set a bedtime of 7.30 for your three-year-old since it doesn't give you enough time.

Similarly, if you need to pick up your husband from the station at 6 o'clock, you'll be pushed to start your eight-month-old's bedtime routine at 6.30. So make sure you set a time which will help you to get on with that routine in a relaxed fashion.

As a rough rule of thumb, the following bedtimes are recommended:

Under 3 years: before 6.00
Under 5: before 7.00
Under 7: before 7.30

Under 10: before 8.00
Under 13: before 8.30
Under 15: before 9.00

If your toddler still has a daytime nap, you may need to make evening bedtime later. But beware of making it so late that it gets dangerously close to your own bedtime.

Try shunting that morning nap forwards. Encourage your toddler to go to sleep just before lunch or after. (See also Chapter 9: Breaking the routine.)

After the age of three years keep the nap short and gently wake him after 20 minutes so he'll have enough time to feel sleepy before proper bedtime. Afternoon physical exercise – like a walk or play in the garden – can also help to tire children out so they're ready for bed.

Finally, remember that a good bedtime routine is like giving your child a present for life. You're helping him to establish his independence in a firm but kindly way.

You're also helping him to grow. We all need sleep to refresh our bodies and our minds. Think how bad you feel when you haven't had enough time in bed. And then think how wonderful and on-top-of-the-world you feel when you *have*.

Wouldn't you like to help your child to feel the same? Then remember, it *is* possible!

· *Paul* ·

At five years old, Paul was a real slowcoach at bedtime. As soon as the word 'bed' was mentioned, he would slow down. He was slow to finish his tea and slow to go upstairs, slow to undress and slow to wash. His parents were very patient and felt that it was important for Paul to express his personality. But as he grew older Paul became slower and slower and his parents became progressively more annoyed. Then Granny came to stay for a few nights. She was very surprised at Paul's behaviour because he was quite normal and active during the day. She devised some games to help Paul to speed up. Each game seemed to work for one or two nights and then Paul's parents would have to use something else. The games they played included piggyback up the stairs, counting to three and expecting Paul to be in the bath at the end of the counting, chasing into the bath if he didn't make it in time. Other games included the cold water game, with cold water being sprinkled over Paul if he didn't get out of the bath immediately when asked to. Then there was the monster chasing game and the tickling game, which were threatened if he was too slow. Often the games would lead to hoots of laughter, so that in the end Paul might not have got to bed any quicker but it was a whole lot more fun!

· *A good routine: a summary* ·

A routine will only work if parents persist and stick at it until the routine is well established. This may take six months or so. But the benefits will last for years. At times, it may seem tiresome, boring and restrictive. But it has the following advantages:

- Ultimately, there will be *less hassle* with bedtime.
- Your child will become *more predictable*.
- A routine can be made more *flexible* once it's established.
- Your child will get to sleep *faster*.

Example of a bedtime routine for John, aged 11 months

4.30. Tea.

5.00. Quiet play with toys.

5.30. Tidy away toys. John 'helps' by posting some of his shapes into a shape-sorting toy.

5.45. John's mother runs his bath and undresses him.

6.00. Bathtime over. John's mother dries him and sings a counting song: 'One, two, three, four, five'. At the same time, she dries each relevant toe and finger before dressing John in his pyjamas.

6.15. She dims the light and draws the curtains.

6.30. John's mother tucks him up in bed, gives him his comforter.

6.40. She says a prayer or nursery rhyme with him, with actions. 'God Bless John' (she points to John), 'Mummy' (she points to herself), etc.

6.50. John's mother turns out the light, goes out and shuts the door.

Example of a bedtime routine for Amy, aged two years, and Tim, aged nine months

5.00. Tea.

5.30. Quiet play with toys. Amy helps her father to clear away the toys. He helps her to read the sitting-room clock and says it's half-past five. He takes her and Tim upstairs.

5.45. Bathtime. Amy's father helps Amy to put toy ducks in the bath. When she splashes around too much, he tells her to 'shhhhh' as it's nearly time for the ducks to go to bed. He baths Tim at the same time.

6.00. Amy's father dries Tim in the bathroom and puts him in his baby seat while he dries Amy and puts her in her pyjamas. They look at the clock on the bedroom wall. She can't tell the time yet but he points out the paper marker which he has stuck on the clock. Amy can see that the little hand is on the six and the big hand on the 12. She knows that this is bedtime.

6.05. Amy's father reads her a story while she sits up in bed. He carries Tim into the room in his baby seat so he can watch him at the same time.

6.15. He hands Amy her special bedtime bear – Reg – who lives at the end of the bed.

6.20. Amy's father kisses her and says, 'Goodnight, sleep tight.' This is their special phrase.
He goes out of the room and leaves the door slightly ajar. Amy doesn't like it completely shut.

6.25. Tim's daddy reads him a short nursery rhyme and gives him his special bedtime comfort blanket.

6.30. He puts him in his cot, says, 'Goodnight, sleep tight' and goes out of the room, shutting the door. Tim hasn't learned to be afraid of the dark.

At first, Amy's routine went wrong.

7.00. Amy came into the kitchen. Her father was cooking supper. He said 'Bedtime' and walked her back to her room, holding her in front of him but without giving her a cuddle. He knew there was nothing wrong with her.

7.15. Amy came into the kitchen again. Her father did exactly the same as he did before. But he looked her in the eye and sounded very firm.

7.15–7.30. Amy cried in her bed. Her father sat on the steps outside, without letting her see him.

7.35. Amy started crying again. Her father sat outside the room but in such a position that she couldn't see him.

7.55. Amy stopped crying.

8.00. Amy's father peeped round the door. The bed was positioned in such a way that he could see her easily. She was fast asleep. He went downstairs.

After six days like this, Amy settled down into a calmer routine. Although she didn't go to sleep immediately, she stopped coming out of the room because she knew she'd only be returned to bed.

• Chapter Three •

Keeping your child in his cot or bed

Keeping your baby in his cot should not be a problem. It has, after all, four sides. So he shouldn't be able to get out until he's a bit bigger. This is usually between 15 months and two years. But if your child is particularly tall or adept at shinning down cot bars, it might be sooner.

The longer you can keep your child in his cot, the better! It's like strapping him into a pushchair or highchair. You know he's safe.

Those four walls around the cot are an important psychological barrier. They reinforce that 'psychological lock' on the bedroom door which we'll be discussing in the rest of this chapter.

However, there will come a time when your child will be able to climb over the side. This can obviously be dangerous. If he does this:

- Lower the side bar.

- Put a mattress beside the cot to cushion him in case he falls.

- Always make sure the room is safe. If he gets out without your realising, he shouldn't be able to harm himself.

- Think about buying him a bed.

· *Bertie* ·

Bertie's parents had worked hard at getting the bedtime routine well established and by the time he was three years old, he really enjoyed his preparation for bed. The problems started as soon as his parents said goodnight, turned the light off and went out of the room. Almost immediately Bertie would be out of bed and come out of his room to see what his parents were doing. It seemed as though this had also become part of his routine now. Bertie's parents had recently taken him out of a cot and put him in a bed and this seemed to be the cause of the trouble. The decided that they would put him back in the cot even though he was getting quite large for it. This worked well but Bertie enjoyed jumping up and down in the cot and moving around a lot as if he were exercising. His parents thought this was probably normal and the health visitor agreed. However, because he was getting large, there was concern that he might climb out of his cot and fall on the floor. The health visitor suggested putting a mattress or some cushions or several layers of blankets on the floor to break Bertie's fall in case he did come over the side while practising his gymnastics. Sure enough, six weeks later this happened. There was a terrific crash in the middle of the night and screams from Bertie. Fortunately, he didn't even have a bruise. Nevertheless, Bertie's parents were not going to risk another fall and they decided to leave him in the cot but take the cot side down. After two weeks of this they transferred him to an ordinary bed. Bertie had got used to sleeping in a cot with no sides and not getting out so he made no effort to get out of the bed.

· *Making that step from cot to bed* ·

Many parents worry that when their toddler progresses from a cot to a bed, there won't be a physical barrier to stop him getting out of it. Encourage him to stay put by:

- Starting as you mean to go on. As soon as you catch him getting out, say 'No, bed!' in a firm, meaningful way. And put him back into bed.

- Choosing a bed design with slightly raised, solid sides to discourage him from falling over the edge when he's asleep. And they will make it slightly more difficult for him to leap in and out.

- Presenting the bed idea as another step up that growing-up ladder. Tell your child that he is such a good, grown-up, clever boy that he is going to have his or her own bed. Isn't that wonderful? You could have fun choosing a new duvet cover. Perhaps you could rearrange the room so it's a novelty to go to bed. And stay there . . .

- If you buy a bed guard, make sure it conforms to British Standards or similar European safety standards. Check that your child can't get his head trapped between the bars.

- If you're short of space, think carefully about the pros and cons of bunk beds. These may be more suitable when your child is older (five plus) and used to staying in bed. Some children find it scary to be in the top bunk – and can indeed fall out. Others don't always like being 'down below' because of feeling shut in by the bed above.

· *Be strong!* ·

Now comes the tricky bit. If you have the kind of child who leaps out of bed or yells as soon as your back is turned, it's tempting to pick him up and take him downstairs so you can get on with your own supper or sort out another child.

But be strong! Think about giving him that present for life. To be able to be content with your own company and to have a feeling of inner security and confidence is a gift indeed.

First, check that your child's room is still safe. We can't emphasise too strongly how important this is. Has your child opened a wardrobe door or pulled out his toys since you put him down to bed. No? Then there's no reason why he shouldn't be put straight back into a safe environment – and why we shouldn't expect him to stay there.

Secondly, is your child ill? This is always something you should think about when your child is upset at night. Does he have a temperature? Is he hot? Does he have a rash? Has he been sick?

Children who are ill tend to be quieter than normal although they may also be more demanding. It can sometimes be difficult to tell when a child is ill, so it is useful to have a thermometer in the house. Always check with your family doctor if you are not sure.

If your child is well and his room is safe, it's perfectly reasonable for you to expect him to stay in his room. Does that sound hard? Then try seeing it this way. Do you feel confident about walking down the street with your child and being sure that he won't run into the road? If you *are* sure, how did you achieve that? The answer is likely to be because you have drummed in the message that he has to stay by you otherwise it's dangerous.

Leaving your child alone

An essential part of growing up is learning to be alone. The first step in this process is learning to be alone in bed at night. The special advantage of this is that you know your child is safe in bed and the darkness helps your child to feel alone. If children do not learn to be confident alone then they will end up feeling lonely and we all know how unpleasant that is.

Learning to be alone does not cause psychological harm. It is children who have not learned to be alone who have the problems. By leaving your child alone in the bedroom you are helping him to know how to be alone. You are also helping him to take the first steps in learning how to develop self control. He will discover that he does not need to be with Mummy all the time in order to be safe. He will find that if he controls his urge to be cuddled and comforted all the time he will be safe and secure during the night. He will know that there is a time and place for cuddles and comfort.

Learning to be alone is a gradual process which continues throughout a child's life. So it is best if the first steps are taken early on when parents can control the process and when they know that their child is absolutely safe. *The New Baby and Toddler Sleep Programme* is a good opportunity to help your child in the first steps towards the self confidence and inner security that we all aim for.

Now you can use the same psychological approach to keep your child in his room. Obviously a lorry isn't going to run over your child if he walks down the stairs after bedtime. But tell yourself it's just as important. Your conviction will rub off on him. And it *is* important. It's that vital step to independence and growth.

If your child has not learned to stay on the pavement safely, you need more practice. Just as you need to encourage your child to stay in his room. Encouraging your child to stay in his room and stay on the pavement are both examples of how you can help your child to control himself. The only way children learn self-control is by being controlled from the outside first.

Training and Routine are the key words. Get into that bedtime routine as soon as you can. And put Training into practice by praising and rewarding your child for following it. (See the section on Rewards on page 139.)

· *Babies' cries* ·

When a baby cries, it's natural for us as parents to respond by picking him up, cuddling or feeding. Crying awakens very powerful emotions in us. We want to protect our children. That's only natural and right.

A newborn baby's cries should never be ignored. Most parents would find it impossible anyway. But you're still getting to know your baby. You're not sure exactly why he is crying. And until you can work that out, you won't be able to relax.

Try running through the following checklist.

- Is he hungry?
- Is he damp?
- Is he too hot/cold?
- Is he ill?
- Is he in pain?

Did you know?

New-born babies have a natural sleep cycle of about 20 minutes, followed by 20 minutes awake. Adults have a sleep cycle of about three hours, and the knack is to learn to drift back into another cycle without waking up fully. The same is true for babies.

Don't be surprised if your baby wakes every 20 minutes or so, because this is normal. It is also normal for a young baby to fall asleep after about 20 minutes awake, so you may need to wake the baby up during feeds. Don't take it personally that he has dozed off while you were feeding him.

TIP: If your baby stops crying almost as soon as you pick him up, there is probably not much wrong with him. If you are still not sure, try picking him up again when he cries and see what happens. If he stops again, you can be reassured that it can't be too serious.

If your baby continues to cry, try the following:

- Hold your baby against your shoulder and sway from side to side, patting his back very gently. Alternatively, bring the car seat into the house, strap him in and rock it gently in your arms. The swaying movement often sends children to sleep. Best of all, put him in a baby sling strapped to your body and then rock him to sleep.

- Sing gently. Lullabies were a wonderful invention! Many adults still recall the lullabies their mothers sang to them and pass them on to their own children. The soft sound of a familiar parent's voice is often enough to lull your child to sleep.

- Other sounds. Turn the vacuum cleaner on. The low hum will often reassure a baby. Even better, make your own low humming noise which you can control yourself instead of having to rely on a machine. Some parents use a 'white music' tape.

  Any repetitive sound such as a ticking clock, a vacuum cleaner or a washing machine, can have a soothing effect.

But . . .

The problem with all these sounds and movements is that your baby might become hooked on them and won't settle until you have gone through a whole performance! To avoid this happening, watch out for the first signs of drowsiness and drooping eyelids. Then put your baby in the cot, carrying on with the sounds and movements as you do so.

If your baby starts to cry almost immediately, just going with your quiet humming and movement as little as possible. If your baby finds that he c any change in his small world by crying, he bored and give up.

Gradually, you'll find that you naturally to cry for slightly longer periods as he g baby is brand-new and cries, you'll stop and turn to him immediately. If he's a f old, you might finish your conversati learn about your own child before taki almost an art form to know when to other hand, it would be unreasonable to expect your under-six-month old baby to sleep through the night without waking and crying once in a while.

· *Older babies and toddlers* ·

Eventually, there comes a point when you have to decide if you're always going to do this to get your baby to sleep. Will you be standing there, crooning to your eight-year-old and if so, what will you be doing when he is 18? If you don't mind, that's fine. But if you do, you'll have to find a way of phasing it out.

Now comes the difficult bit. You've put your older baby or toddler into his cot and he shows his objections by yelling or trying to get out.

Before you go rushing in, remember that the cot has sides. There should be no problem in leaving him in the cot, provided you know he is safe and well. If you have done all you can to check all is well and you have gone through the calming routine, then it is quite reasonable to let him cry.

However, crying – and the thorny question of whether you should leave him to cry or not – is such a big issue that it needs a chapter to itself (see the following chapter). Here, we'll start with what you should do if your child 'escapes' ...d!

· *In and out of bed* ·

...uickly as you can. It is best to do this before ...ut of his room. If he sees all the exciting ...g in the rest of the house, he'll be even ... do a U-turn. But remember. You're in ... back to bed.

...on't try to reason. You're an adult and ...stify your actions. (It's one of the few perks in parenting!) Phrases like 'You'll be tired in the morning', 'I need to cook supper' or a simple 'Back to bed' will do. There's less scope for him to argue back – and even a 15-month-old can do that!

- *Look firm.* Are you saying 'No' but looking sympathetic too? Then it's not surprising if your child is getting the wrong message. Make sure you look as though you mean what you are saying.

  Everyone has a special look that says, 'I have had quite enough of this. I am really serious now!'

  If you don't think you have developed the art of this look, ask your partner. It would be surprising if you have never used it on him or her . . .

- *Sound firm.* You don't have to be hard or dragon-like but you do have to be firm. Simply utter the word 'Bed' with conviction. You mean it. And you have to make sure that he knows you mean it. It helps to put extra emphasis on the beginning and end of words.

- *Use firm gestures.* Back up what you say with a definite and clear gesture. Point clearly to the bed in such a way that leaves no doubt what is meant. Have you ever seen Italian police directing the traffic? They use simple and often graceful gestures. They are so clear and firm that no one dares to ignore them.

· *Sally* ·

Sally was a very easy baby and as she grew older s[...]
well behaved, that is until she was three and d[...]
infection and had to be admitted to hospital.[...]
unsettle her and when she returned home [...]
during the night and cried out for her [...]
surprise them because they knew that S[...]
worried and lonely in hospital. They did e[...]
reassure her and were very quick to resp[...]
did not go into her room immediately, Sal[...]

and go into the parents' room. After a few months the crying stopped but the wakefulness and coming into the parents' bedroom continued. By the age of four and a half, Sally was regularly getting up during the night and getting into bed on her father's side. She had obviously worked out that he was much less likely to take her back to bed than her mother was. After several more months of disturbed nights, the parents decided that they must do something about it. They decided that because Sally's mother was more able to be firm with her, she would be the one to take Sally back to her room. They rearranged the furniture so it was impossible for Sally to get round to father's side of the bed without her waking both of them. Sally's mother found that if she held Sally very firmly and marched her straight back to bed saying sharply, 'Go back to bed immediately', with a serious and determined look on her face, Sally would go back to bed quite easily. If Sally's mother said the usual goodnight phrase, then she seemed to go back to sleep very quickly. Sally's father felt rather resentful that his wife seemed to be so much more effective than he was. In fact, because he felt she was a bit too strict, he tended to try to compensate for that by being softer and more easy-going. However, because the parents realised that their different styles of discipline were also causing problems during the day, the father agreed to try to be firmer. His wife taught him how to use his facial expression, his gesture and his voice to make it clear to Sally that he meant what he said. This seemed to work quite well and he realised that it was much better to act the part of the firm father rather than allow himself to be taken advantage of by his ... old daughter, with her taking little notice of what he ... he would have to say it over and over again until ... would lose his temper and shout at her. This made ... ever she was doing and look at her father in a way ... is all the fuss about? Why are you getting so

... ce. If you find this difficult, pretend ... ess. Your toddler is the audience. Play ... e gestures dramatic. 'BED!' If your ... sed, your performance is not good enough. So try again or ask your partner/mother/ sister/friend to do it for you. Learn from them. Can you pick up any acting tips? If you have a very critical audience, you may have to put on an Oscar-winning performance to produce an impression . . .

Seeing it as a play will also defuse the situation. Bedtime is one of the most difficult times for parents because we're all tired at the end of the day. We're less patient. The smallest thing can annoy us. Acting can unwind us and be quite relaxing. You can say to yourself, 'This is not really me – it is only an act. Let's see if I can impress the audience tonight!'

- Pretend that this child who won't go to bed isn't really yours. Sounds odd? Think about it. Supposing you're looking after a friend's child for the night and he won't go back to bed. Would you tear him off a strip? Probably not. But you'd still be firm in a kind way. Do the same with your own child.

- Avoid the word 'please'. It's surprisingly easy to beg your child to do what you're telling him. And that would be giving him the wrong message. You're in charge. Remember?

· *He's off!* ·

If your child is quick, he may well have beaten you to it. Before you know it, he's out of his bedroom and down the stairs.

- Don't chase him. The best reaction is not to give him much attention but still get him back to his room. If you run after him, you're going to give him plenty of attention. He might well enjoy the chase! Don't say anything but walk calmly up to him. And then catch him.

- Resist the temptation to talk to him. Again, the less attention, the better. He's not really there…

- Don't look at him. He should be in bed, not running around. If you pay him as little attention as possible, he may work out that it's not worth his while to get up all the time.

- Walk him back, in front of you. Don't pick him up for a cuddle. Why should he want to go back to bed if he can stay up and cuddle you instead? Again, this may sound hard but it depends on how serious you are. If you walk with him just in front of you, he'll know you mean business. And you do. Don't you? You're in charge. Remind yourself of that.

- Use a firm hold. How you hold your child will give a clear message. A gentle cuddle means 'I am enjoying this'. A firm hold means 'I mean what I say'. An uncomfortable hold means 'I am completely fed up'. There is no need to cause any pain. This will only increase the crying and cause delay in going to sleep. Your hold should communicate that you are firm and determined.

Now take him back to bed, say 'Goodnight' firmly using the special words and walk out of the room. If he gets out of bed again, walk him back using the steps already described. Keep going. It's tiring. It's boring. And it's time-wasting. There are so many other things you could – and should – be doing instead, such as making supper or simply relaxing with your partner.

But when you succeed, you'll be earning yourself future evenings of free time to do what you like.

By taking your child back to bed calmly every time, he or you will eventually give up. You have to make sure it's him and not you who gives in. And you *can* decide it. All you have to do is keep going. Soon – it may take three evenings or perhaps a few more – you'll find your child will no longer jump out of bed every time you say goodnight. He'll realise that it's not worth his while.

Why be firm?

Children need to know where the limits are. What they can do and what they can't do. Firm and clear guidelines are a way of keeping children safe. When you teach your child about keeping clear of danger such as fire, electricity, water and heights you cannot afford to be half-hearted about it. It is not something for negotiation or reasoning with long explanations. You will have to be absolutely firm and clear that your child must not put a finger in the electric socket or run out into the street. It is a matter of life and death.

The New Baby and Toddler Sleep Programme provides an opportunity for you to practise being firm in a situation where it is not a matter of life and death. You can practise being firm about bedtime and about your child staying in bed. If it doesn't work then no harm is done and all you need to do is practise a bit more. When you achieve your goal you will know that your child is safer than before.

If you are really determined, your child will learn to do what you say and understand that you really do mean it! When that happens, give yourself a pat on the back. You've succeeded in putting in a 'psychological lock' on your child's bedroom door.

Some parents actually put a simple lock on the door in order to ensure that their toddler is safe in his bedroom and not wandering around the house with the risks posed by gas or electric cookers and heaters/falling down stairs, etc.

On the other hand, locking your child in his room could be a danger in itself if there was a house fire. Each parent has to decide what is in their child's best interests. The benefit of a 'psychological lock' is that your child has learned for himself that he doesn't go through that door until he has your permission.

After you've given yourself a pat on the back, praise your child too. Remember the phrase 'Positive Training,' i.e., training your child to keep within the boundaries and praising him when he does so. Tell him how pleased you are that he stays in bed. If he's old enough, you might even want to reward him in some way for good behaviour.

· *Thomas* ·

Thomas had eventually settled down and learnt to go to sleep in an ordinary bed when he was three. However he was an active boy and from the age of four he started to get out of bed at night and roam around the house. This was all right before his parents went to bed because they heard him creeping about and were able to take him straight back to bed. It was different during the night because they were both deep sleepers. Sometimes, they would wake to find Thomas sitting downstairs in front of the television at 3 a.m. They wondered whether he had been sleepwalking but the GP told them that this was very unlikely because sleepwalkers only carry out very simple tasks and they usually stay deeply asleep. Naturally, Thomas's parents were worried that he might come to some harm, as he wandered around in the middle of the night. They put a stairgate in his doorway and this worked for a while but he soon learnt to climb over it. His parents were so worried about him that they decided to lock Thomas in his room because they thought that this was the safest thing to do. In fact they used a simple hook and screw eye to keep the door shut. It was just strong enough to prevent Thomas opening the door but was easy to force if they wanted to get in, in a hurry. Soon, however, Thomas was strong enough to pull the hook out, so his parents had to think again. This time they decided to install a burglar alarm with an infrared movement detector to cover the stairs and part of the landing. They explained to Thomas what they had done, but he took no notice and then got a terrible shock when he came out of his room in the middle of the night and tried to go downstairs. The surprise was so great that Thomas never tried it again.

· *It doesn't work* ·

This is all very well in theory. But what if it doesn't work for you? Supposing:

'My child starts crying' (see also next chapter)

It sounds hard. But if you really want to establish a good sleeping pattern, you have to help your child to learn that crying will not bring you back. He has to learn that when he goes to bed, he goes to sleep. He's not there to play the game of Trap the Parent! This game involves finding and getting a parent back into the bedroom. Extra points are awarded for speed of arrival and the length of time a parent stays. The child gets a bonus point if the parent brings something in (like a drink) for his child.

Absurd? Maybe, maybe not! Perhaps your child is just plain lonely. But whatever he's thinking, if you come in and pick him up, he'll know what to do. He'll cry the next night so you come in again. And the next.

As a result, he won't learn how to go to sleep on his own. He'll always need you. Perhaps you don't mind that. But if you do, turn to the next chapter.

'My child is scared of the dark'

If you start early enough, there's no reason why this should happen. After all, your baby was in the womb for nine months. And there weren't any electric light bulbs there!

Of course, complete darkness makes it more difficult for you to check on your baby or for your older child to find his way to the lavatory. But it is still better for the light to be on outside the bedroom and under your control.

You could also see it another way. If you leave a light on, you're giving the message that dark is dangerous. A fear of the dark is natural. Everyone has to be careful in the dark: it's easy to bump into things or trip over. But darkness itself is not dangerous.

Dark is not dangerous

If you child is safely tucked up in bed then there is no danger from being in darkness. It is only when children wander around in the dark that they might trip over something or bump into furniture. That is one of the reasons why you need to make sure that your child's room is totally safe.

Children who learn to cope in the dark will have gained another skill and will be all the more confident for it. Blind people do not get anxious because their world is dark. In fact they gain other skills and abilities which most of us don't have to cope with every day life.

The New Baby and Toddler Sleep Programme helps children to become confident in the dark and as a result gain extra coping skills.

It may be a basic instinct to be afraid of the dark as, in former times, it would have been dangerous to have gone out at night and risk being hurt by wild animals. But this does not happen in the bedroom – which, by now, you've made sure is totally safe. Children need to know they are safe in their bed at night in the dark. The only way they can find this out is by trying it out and keeping the room dark.

TIP: Pretend, with your toddler, that his bed is like a ship. It's a safe place to be. Close your eyes and you can almost hear the sea . . .

Sadly, many adults are still not happy about being in darkness at night because they were scared of the dark as children. So, if your child is still a baby, start as you mean to go on. Otherwise it will be difficult to prevent this fear of the dark from developing.

If you don't start this routine until later and your child has already developed a fear of the dark, you could 'wean' him off this fear by using an electric plug-in nightlight or leave the landing light on. Another idea is lower-watt bulbs or any other safe way of shielding light from your child.

As your child gets more used to going to bed, start leaving lights off or use a dimmer switch. The idea is to help him to feel comfortable without any extra help. It's yet another step on that ladder to self-dependence and self-confidence.

Did you know?

There's also another fascinating chemical fact about darkness. Your child's pineal gland – and yours too – naturally produces the substance melatonin. The release of this hormone is stimulated by the darkness. In other words, more of this chemical is produced when the room is dark. Melatonin is actually a natural sedative and automatically quietens the body down in preparation for sleep. So, by encouraging your child to accept the dark, you're doing him a favour. You're also encouraging the production of melatonin which will make him want to rest.

Amazing, isn't it?

'My child will only sleep in my bed'

Some research shows that cot death is possibly less likely to occur if young babies sleep in a parent's bedroom during the first few weeks or months. (See pages 134–5 for more information on cot death.)

However, this can lead to problems if it continues for too long. Research also shows that parents and children who share the same room or bed – often known as co-sleeping – *both* wake up more. So neither of you will get the rest you need.

Of course, it isn't easy. Toddlers and even older babies can learn to dislike bedtime so much that they will only go to sleep in Mummy and Daddy's bed. Sometimes we're just as much to blame for this. If your child won't stay in bed, it's tempting to lie down with them if only to shut your own tired eyes after a hard day! It's also tempting to do this on your own bed which is probably bigger and more comfortable.

The danger is that your baby, and most certainly your toddler, will get used to this. It's nice to have someone lying next to you. You know that yourself if you are in a steady happy relationship with a cosy double bed.

If you don't mind the idea of your child being in your bed for the next four years or so, that's up to you. But if you *do*, then do something about it fast before the habit sticks! Ask yourself who makes the rules in your family. Do you or does your child have the final say?

Some parents try to have the best of both worlds by lying down with their child, waiting until he's asleep and then gently carrying him over to his own bed. The obvious disadvantage is that when your child wakes in the night and realises you are no longer there, he's more likely to come and find you! But if he's used to going down on his own, he'll probably turn over and go back to sleep again.

It's also tempting to let your child doze off in front of the television after the bathtime routine. Again, this is more of an adult habit than a child's one! In the short term, it seems more convenient for you. You can watch your favourite programme instead of sitting upstairs with your child and hearing the title music. And you don't feel you're missing out on that precious evening time with your partner.

But the drawback in allowing your child to fall asleep in the sitting room is that, like all habits, your child will soon get used to it. Why should he suddenly start going to bed after his bath when he's been accustomed to coming downstairs with you?

You can see his point! It goes back to that old phrase 'Start as you mean to go on', however difficult it seems in the first place!

Think of it this way. At some point, your child has to learn to go to bed on his own. He can't still expect you to lie down with him when he's 10 years old or a teenager – just as you wouldn't expect him to be wearing nappies at that age. The longer you leave it, the harder it will be for both of you to break the habit.

If, that is, you want to.

'My child won't allow me to leave the room without crying or screaming'

Who is in charge? It's a question we've asked before. But it really is at the hub of this problem. If you are in charge – and you should be at your age – you can teach your child not to cry any more.

Start by teaching yourself the difference in your child's various cries. You can learn to distinguish between cries that signal:

- Real distress
- Anger
- Attention-seeking/demands
- Teething
- Automatic habit

You can do this by listening carefully throughout your child's life to the cries which he makes in different situations. It's almost like cracking a secret code.

If you think the cry comes from:

- **Pain/discomfort** The cause may be obvious – but if not you need to seek professional advice.

- **Separation anxiety** Remember this is normal and natural. Try to get your child used to being separated from you for short periods during the day. Do it gradually.

Start by leaving the room for a short time before coming back. This can be extended into short trips out, away from your child so you both get used to being without each other.

Gradual daytime separations will help your child to become used to being separated from you at night.

● **Anger**   Ask yourself what your child is angry about. Is it reasonable or is it an automatic habit because you're not there? Check by going in and seeing if the crying stops. If it does, your child is more likely to be playing you up. But if the crying continues when you're there, he's more likely to be crying from real distress and not just anxiety or anger.

· *Darren* ·

Darren had cried quite a lot as a baby but his parents had persevered and eventually they managed to get him settled into a good sleep routine when he was 18 months old. All went well until he was two and a half and then for no apparent reason he started to refuse to go to bed at night and would wake during the night, crying out for Mummy. The parents went through a checklist of what could be wrong with Darren. Was he ill, was it teething, colic, pain, discomfort, loneliness, a nightmare? It wasn't at all clear. They had noticed that Darren had become more clingy during the day and that it was difficult to leave him alone for more than a few moments. He cried every time they took him to the day nursery and screamed when they left. The health visitor suggested that Darren might have separation anxiety. This normally starts to develop between six to eight months and can become a problem from 18 months onwards. The health visitor suggested that Darren should have experience of happy separations. This meant teaching him that he could manage on his own by leaving him for progressively longer periods. They did this during the day by leaving Darren with a friend for a few minutes before returning and then gradually building up on this. At night-time the parents operated the same system by leaving Darren in bed for a longer and longer time before returning full of praise and encouragement.

· *What to do?* ·

There are two approaches: rapid and gradual.

Rapid   You could let your child cry (see also next chapter). After all, you've already checked there is nothing wrong with him.

Gradual   You could:

- Stay in the room with your child and gradually decrease the amount of time you are there.

For a fuller explanation, see the next chapter: Leaving your child to cry.

> TIP: Give older toddlers a simple practical reason why you have to go out of the room. Explain that you need to turn off the cooker. Your child might be more likely to accept a practical reason for your departure. Although he could then come and look for you when you don't return . . .

'I usually spend about 20 minutes with my child at night before going out of the room. Is that too long?
It might be worth asking yourself if the problem lies with you. Are you lonely? Is your partner out or not there at all? If so, perhaps it's time to develop some independence yourself downstairs.

Alternatively, are you afraid of something? If so, what? Your child is well and his bedroom is safe.

Try thinking about your child. He needs that time alone to rest and grow. So you are helping him by giving him that time.

· *Lisa* ·

Lisa was three years old and really enjoyed being read to last thing at night. The only problem was, the longer the story the more likely she was to wake up at night. After discussing the problem with friends, Lisa's parents realised this was not unusual and that toddlers often sleep less well if they have spent a long time with the parent before going to sleep. As she had grown older Lisa had become more and more demanding and her parents now had to read a whole book before she would allow them to stop. Although Lisa's parents wanted her to learn as much as possible from the books they read to her, they decided they would have to limit the reading – they decided to limit it to five minutes. They explained this to Lisa and used a cooking timer to 'ping' when the time was up. They then offered to read at a normal speed or they could read very very fast and finish the book in five minutes, before the 'pinger' went if Lisa would prefer that. After hearing her father read at speed and not being able to understand any of it, Lisa opted for the ordinary reading rate over the five minutes. Her parents were surprised how well she accepted this. Perhaps she realised that her parents were quite determined to keep the time short after they discovered that Lisa did sleep better during the night when they spent less time with her once she was in bed.

'I haven't time to keep taking my child back'

Of course you haven't. Not many parents have. You've got other children to look after. You've got the house to sort out. And you're exhausted.

The answer is to make the rest of your life as simple as possible. Prepare a simple supper in advance because you know you won't have much time to spend in the kitchen. Keep your other children occupied with books, games or a suitable video if necessary. Let the house stay untidy for a few evenings until you've got your child into this routine you're working towards. It's only for a short period of time. When you've succeeded, you'll have your evenings back again. But if you give up, you'll lose those precious evenings for several years to come.

If you are a single parent, it can be really difficult. Have you got a friend or relative who could come and help you? If there are two of you at home, you could take it in turns to run the bedtime routine. Or better still, do it together.

Two parents both putting on an act of total determination should be very impressive. If it isn't, you may have problems. How are you going to control your child at other times when it might be a dangerous situation? Perhaps you both need some acting lessons to improve your performance. If one of your friends seems to be able to make an impression on children, ask him/her for tips.

'My partner comes home just when I've got my child to bed'

Infuriating, isn't it? It's hardly surprising that the sound of the key turning in the lock or the doorbell makes your toddler leap out of bed to see Mummy or Daddy. So work out a plan with your partner. Perhaps it's best if he comes in quietly and doesn't see his son. Sounds tough? The alternative would be to say goodnight briefly and then pay for it by your child wanting to be up all evening. Wouldn't it be better for him to have a rested night and then give your partner more quality time – maybe alone – with your child at weekends?

Alternatively, you might prefer to follow the usual bedtime wind-down ritual until you hear your partner returning. Don't get as far as saying goodnight to your child. Get your partner to calmly finish off the routine. And then he or she can say the goodnight bit and walk out of the room.

The disadvantage is that this brief appearance might not be enough. Your child might want to see more of Mummy or Daddy who has been out all day. So if this doesn't work, you may need to get your partner to take over the Go To Bed routine at weekends when he or she is home.

'What if my child is ill?'

Clearly, the routine may have to change if your child is ill. He'll want to doze off during the day which means he won't be so keen to sleep at night.

Nevertheless, the bedtime routine can be very reassuring for a sick child. Even though your child may feel very strange, at least the routine is familiar and predictable.

As we've already explained, going to bed doesn't necessarily mean going to *sleep*. It can mean having a rest. If your poorly toddler is awake at eight o'clock in the evening and really can't sleep because he had a nap at 6 p.m., don't worry because the rest will do him good. However, you may need to check more often to see what you can do to make him more comfortable.

Ill children need lots of extra love and attention. But as soon as your child starts to get better, go back to your original routine. Don't wait until he's fully recovered as the longer the gap, the more difficult it will be to return to normality.

'My child is too tired to sleep'

It's true that some children get to a stage where they're over-tired. They're beyond sleep. They're exhausted and irritable with it! They may throw temper tantrums. They're beyond reason. Even the normal comforters won't pacify them.

Remember that tired children become hyperactive and disobedient. The bedtime routine is particularly helpful for the overtired child. Once the routine is well established, a tired child will just slot in and follow it automatically. In any case, it is not the sleep which is so important. The goal is for your child to be quietly in bed. Sleep will then come – eventually.

· *The hyperactive child* ·

It's often difficult getting any child to bed. But if your child is hyperactive, it can be even harder. The key is to remember that these children lack self-control. They are often bright as well but they usually have an immaturity which needs extra control from the outside.

This sleeping programme is all about controlling your child in a kind but firm way and will help to reduce the hyperactivity.

To help a hyperactive child go to bed – even if it's to rest rather than sleep – just do more of the same. In other words, do what we've already advised, but do more of it.

Try:

- Giving him more routine. Do things in the same order as you draw closer to bedtime. Let it become an almost hypnotic, reassuring sequence of events which comforts him.

- Be consistent. Do what you say you'll do. Don't do one thing one evening and something else on another evening.

- Be kind but firm.

· *Jamie* ·

Jamie had always been a very active and restless child. As he grew older and mixed with other children it became obvious that he had less self-control than other children. He was clumsy and could not concentrate for long. He had never slept well but did not wake his parents up in the night. He either played quietly in bed or ranged around the room and if he slept through the night the bedclothes were in a complete muddle in the morning. When Jamie was five years old and had just started school his teacher complained about his over-activity. Jamie was clumsy and disruptive. He was so impulsive that it seemed as though he was driven by a high-

powered engine somewhere inside him. A GP referred Jamie to the child psychiatrist who diagnosed Attention Deficit and Hyperactivity Disorder (ADHD). Jamie's parents were told that this condition occurred more commonly in boys, tended to run in families and that the main cause was developmental immaturity that affected the ability to have self-control. The parents were given exercises for Jamie which involved them providing more external control for him at first and then teaching him to take control of himself, at first for short periods and then for increasingly longer periods. They were told that diet was unlikely to be a cause of Jamie's hyperactivity but the control that was involved in going on a diet seemed to help some children. The parents asked about drug treatment for the condition and were told that there were a number of drugs available but they only dealt with the symptoms of the disorder and were not usually prescribed under the age of seven. In the end Jamie had to learn to control his attention and his impulses for himself and there was a good chance that hard work at this stage would help him to grow out of the problem. The big concern with Jamie's age was that he should not get behind with reading as this would only increase his difficulties at school. In fact teaching Jamie to read, which involved getting him to sit in one place and concentrate for short periods using lots of encouragement, praise and rewards, was just the type of help that Jamie would benefit from most. Over the next year Jamie's parents and his class teacher worked very hard to help him and gradually his behaviour improved. His parents were interested to see that as Jamie gained more self-control his sleep improved and the bedclothes were less disturbed when they came in to wake him up in the morning.

'There's so much noise in the house that my child wants to see what's going on'

Life goes on, doesn't it? You can't stop the other children talking or stop the phone ringing because your child needs to go to sleep. Resist the temptation to creep around. Your child needs to get used to normal sounds of life around him. The sooner you do this when he's a baby, the sooner he'll get used to it.

'I have problems with my personal life and I think my children are picking up on that'

Children are adept at sniffing out secrets. Especially if they're the kind of secrets you'd rather they didn't know about. Sadly, children *do* pick up on emotional disturbances in the home. And this can interfere with their sleeping. It is only natural that if you are close to your child, he will pick up your feelings. It is best to give a simple explanation that is as reassuring as possible.

We're not pretending there are any easy answers. There aren't. But being a parent carries a responsibility. If you remember your own parents arguing or being upset over something, you'll know how much it hurt. As a parent, you are older and wiser than your children so it's up to you not to worry them with adult troubles. Find a quiet space or time to yourself where you can be upset without anyone seeing. It's not easy, but it's worth it, in the long run. Also, try to find a friend or relative who can support you through a difficult time.

'I feel so annoyed with my child that I want to smack him when he gets out of bed'

It's understandable. But don't. You'll work him up and you'll work yourself up. You'll get away from that calm, measured you're-going-back-to-bed walk which we described earlier on. So take a deep breath. And repeat those steps.

Smacking is rather like taking out a bank loan. It may help you in a crisis. But the cost is high as you will have to pay it back – and with interest. The guilt you may feel after smacking can easily make you over-indulgent next time your child is being difficult. (For more on smacking, see Chapter 8.)

'I feel like giving up'

Don't! If at first you don't succeed, try and try again. As parents, we can help our children to get through difficult areas in life by showing them, through our actions, that it *is* possible to go on, even when things are difficult.

If you give up, you'll be doing two things. You'll be telling your child it's 'all right' to give in when the going is tough. And you'll be encouraging him to assume that you'll back down in other areas (eating/holding your hand as you go down the road/going to school) when he doesn't want to do what he's told.

In a world where everything seems to change all the time and there is so much uncertainty, it is reassuring for children to know that there can be continuity and predictability. It helps them to feel secure.

'I can't reason with my child when I say he has to stay in bed'

Then don't! Children under the age of eight have not really reached the age of reason. Their system of logic is different from anyone else's. So stick to practicalities and give simple explanations.

· *Alan* ·

Alan was four years old and very bright. He was always questioning his parents and asking them 'why...'? When he started asking his parents why he had to go to sleep they usually managed to find a way round it and at first he was satisfied by simple answers. Then one night Alan decided that he really wanted to know why he should go to bed. After quite a long discussion he was persuaded that it was so that he could go to sleep. He then asked for the reason why he had to go to sleep. His parents, who had always been keen to answer Alan's questions, tried to find an answer that would satisfy him. It had taken several hours to get him up to his bedroom and by now it was 9 o'clock. By midnight Alan was becoming rather drowsy but he was still not persuaded by his parents' reasoning about why he needed to go to sleep. His parents had somehow managed to persist with the reasoning for three hours and were at breaking point themselves. Fortunately, Alan drifted off to sleep not long afterwards and his parents decided that they would never ever reason with their son in quite the same way again. They had discovered what many parents find out quite soon, which is that reasoning with a four- or five-year-old – or even a child who is quite a lot older – can be very frustrating and a waste of time. This is because the young child's system of logic is very different from that of most adults.

· *Fall-back method* ·

Some children take longer to stop getting out of bed than others. So try the fall-back method of allowing your child to stay in his room but not come out of it.

You might need to do this with a stairgate at the entrance to the room. If so, make sure your child doesn't start climbing over it in a bid for freedom. Obviously, this could be dangerous.

You also need to make sure that the room is still safe. Listen in every now and then to check all is well. But *don't start socialising with him!* Don't offer to read another story or play a game. It's bedtime. If your child wants to stay in his room, so be it. He's still resting. And as we've said earlier, going to bed doesn't necessarily mean going to sleep. It means resting, too.

Eventually, your child will get fed up. Before you know it, you'll look round the corner and see he's fallen asleep. Sometimes he might even be asleep on the floor. Wait five minutes to check he's really asleep and then move him into the warm bed.

If this is not possible without waking him up, then you could put extra clothes on him, keep the room warm and allow him to sleep on the floor if that is where he is most comfortable.

Then make yourself a drink and give yourself a pat on the

back again. Put a sticker on your own star chart! You've done it. But remember, you need to keep doing it. The next night. And the next. And the next. Until finally, you reach an evening when your child stays in bed on his own. Yes. One evening, this *will* happen! The more determined you are about it, the sooner it will be.

• Chapter Four •
Leaving your child to cry

By now, you can see that helping your child to have a good night's rest is a natural progression. As your child grows from being a baby to a toddler and into an older child, your reaction to each sleeping stage will affect the next.

You'll probably have rocked or soothed him to sleep as a baby. When he was a toddler, you might have battled to keep him in his room even if he was not sleeping. Eventually, there comes a time when every parent has to decide that their child should now be in his own bed throughout the night.

· *What should you do when he cries?* ·

You've reached the stage where your child will stay in his room, but he's still yelling or crying for you. Remember:

- *Crying is normal.* It doesn't necessarily mean that something is seriously wrong. As adults, we have many ways of expressing ourselves, such as talking/singing/dancing. But babies only have one method: crying

- *Crying is healthy.* A lusty cry should be very reassuring. Really ill children and children with developmental problems do not cry normally. They are silent or just whimper. Once you have checked that your child is safe and well, you can allow him to air his lungs, strengthen his chest muscles and train his vocal cords for a future life as a pop star, opera singer or town crier!

Often, of course, crying *does* mean that something is wrong, such as a wet nappy/hunger/wind. So it's natural that, as parents, we respond to babies crying. The sound almost gives us a physical pain, doesn't it? Indeed, it's nature's way of prodding parents into checking that everything is all right.

But as our children grow older, we can't continue responding to them as we did when they were babies: we start gradually to delay our response.

The time to start working on crying during the night is when the child is between six months and one year. After the age of two or three, a good sleeping habit is more difficult for a child to achieve. But it's still possible.

After the age of five, it's even harder. But it's still not impossible. In fact, some children don't sleep well *until* they are five because by then, they're at school. The physical exhaustion of a full school day makes them *want* to go to sleep and they'll need that sleep to help them to cope with their busy lives.

But five years is a long time to wait for a good night's sleep!

Yes, you can let your child cry

Imagine what would happen if you responded immediately every time your child cried. He would soon learn that whenever he wanted your attention or wanted anything else all he has to do is cry. We all have to learn to delay gratification. And it is certainly best for children to learn this before they go to school or spend time being looked after by other adults. They will not respond immediately to your child's cries and demands for attention.

The New Baby and Toddler Sleep Programme helps children to learn that parents make the decisions about how their needs will be met. It will teach your child to be confident in you making the right decisions on his behalf. He will learn to trust you because he will discover that even though his demands for your attention have not been met he will wake up safe the next morning.

Letting a child cry as part of *The New Baby and Toddler Sleep Programme* is a way of showing your love and care for your child. It will help him to learn to manage his emotions and know that he is safe and secure in your care even if every demand for attention is not met.

Why is it so difficult to leave your child to cry? It seems unnatural or even cruel not to respond. Crying is a powerful signal of distress. It automatically sparks off strong emotions in anyone who hears it. Parents have particularly strong reactions to their child's cries, although there is considerable individual variation. It is probably impossible not to have an emotional reaction to crying, so it is going against all your natural instincts to leave your child to cry. And that is difficult.

However, good parenting often means going against your natural inclination. It is all too easy to give in to unreasonable demands for a quiet life. Saying 'no' and sticking to the limit you have set can be really difficult. Allowing your child independence and helping in the process of separation usually means going against your normal instinct to keep your child safe and close to you. Leaving your child to cry is part of this separation process. Sooner or later your child will have to learn how to cope alone with his own anxiety about separation.

TIP: The best way of telling if your baby is ill or in pain is not by his crying but by his behaviour. An ill or seriously distressed child will look, behave and sound different. Each child has individual reactions, but generally an ill child is more likely to be:
- pale
- floppy

- less active than normal
- making unusual movements: for example holding or rubbing a painful area, such as an ear or his tummy
- breathing differently – more rapidly or irregularly
- hot, with a raised body temperature – check with a thermometer (children get hot skin with crying, but crying alone does not increase body temperature)
- cold and clammy
- crying differently from normal – often more highly pitched, or whimpering or moaning

· *Three-day sleeping plan* ·

Leaving your child to cry sounds heartless. But look at it another way. If you can help your child to get himself to sleep, you'll be preparing him for life.

If you stick to the following Three-Day Sleeping Plan, there's at least an 80 per cent chance of improvement.

· *Rebecca* ·

Rebecca was three years old and hardly ever slept through the night. She and her younger brother Richard lived alone with their mother. Their parents were divorced and their father came and took them out for the day every other weekend. Rebecca would often sleep with her mother and was often restless and wakeful. She refused to go to bed alone and insisted on staying up until her mother went to bed. It was clear that Rebecca was not getting enough sleep because she was restless, irritable and overactive during the day. The health visitor, the GP and friends had all given the same advice which was that Rebecca should have a proper bedtime routine, a fixed bedtime that mother decided on and should be in her own bed for at least 12 hours if she was going to get enough rest and sleep. Rebecca's mother had tried insisting and then forcing Rebecca to stay in her room at bedtime. However, Rebecca would cry and then scream until her mother felt unable to bear it any longer. On one occasion when the mother had decided to be really tough she allowed Rebecca to shout and scream for an hour and a half. Eventually Rebecca made herself sick. Her mother felt so guilty about what had happened that she took Rebecca into her bed. Rebecca was still not getting enough sleep or rest and continued to be demanding, irritable and hyperactive during the day and her mother had no time for herself in the evening. Eventually, she decided that enough was enough after discussing the problem with a close friend. They agreed that they would work on Rebecca's bad sleeping habit together and the friend agreed to look after Richard for a few nights while Rebecca was learning to sleep in her own bed. They worked out a bedtime routine and wrote it down with the timings for each stage. They also worked out what could possibly go wrong and agreed a plan to deal with every potential problem. If all else failed, mother would phone the friend any time during the night if she felt she was about to give in to Rebecca's screams. They discussed at great length whether or not this was a fair and reasonable thing to do for Rebecca and whether or not it would do her any harm. As it happened the friend had been through a very similar situation with her own daughter who was about the same age as Rebecca. The girl had screamed for two hours on the first night, for one hour the next night and hardly at all on the third night. She now stayed quietly in her room during the night and was better behaved during the day. This encouraged Rebecca's mother to follow the plan through to the end. Before starting the 'in at the deep end' approach, Rebecca's mother and her friend made sure that the bedroom was completely safe and that Rebecca was well. On the first night Rebecca screamed for an hour and was then sick. Her mother came in to the room, cleared up the sick and made Rebecca comfortable with the minimum of fuss and then left the room. The screaming started again and occurred on and off during the next two hours. Fortunately, the neighbours had been warned about what was happening that night so that was one less thing to worry about. At 4 o' clock in the morning Rebecca eventually fell asleep but when the friend phoned at 9 o'clock the next morning Rebecca's mother told her that she was never ever going to go through that type of experience again and she now felt completely exhausted. The friend suggested that she tried it for one more night. This was agreed and the next morning mother woke up and realised that Rebecca had slept through the night. She found this impossible to believe. However, Rebecca continued to sleep through the night and mother and her friend agreed that it must have been that dreadful night when Rebecca screamed so much that actually sorted the problem. It was also surprising to note how much better behaved Rebecca was during the day. She was less irritable and seemed happier and more settled in herself.

Safety first

The rapid settling, three-night approach can only be justified if your child is completely safe and well both physically and psychologically. Here is the checklist:

- How was your child during the day?
- Was he 'off-colour' at all?
- Has he had a temperature recently?
- Has he been particularly anxious during the day?
- Are there any reasons why he might be upset?
- Have you double-checked the room for safety?
- Do you feel well and safe yourself?

If the checklist is all clear then you can go ahead with the 'In at the deep end' three-night approach with confidence.

Here goes!

- Tell your child what is going to happen. Explain that when you have said goodnight, no one will go into his bedroom until the morning.

- Talk it over with the rest of the people in your house: your partner, other children. Explain that this won't be easy. If necessary, tell the neighbours why they might hear your child crying and screaming.

- Make sure that other important adults will back you up. The support of friends and relatives is vital. Try to find somebody who has succeeded by not responding to their child crying out at night. It will reassure you that you are not the only one to try this method.

- Choose a time when you don't need a lot of sleep yourself, such as a Friday and Saturday night when you or your partner aren't working the next day.

- Arrange the room in such a way that you can easily see what your child is doing in the room – without him necessarily spotting you. Make sure his bed is easily seen from the door or put a 'peephole' in the door so you can look in on him or hang a mirror on the wall so you can again see him without him seeing you. You need to be able to check your child without actually going into the room.

TIP: Oil the door hinges so if you do need to open it to check on your child, they won't creak and give you away. If your child spots you, he'll want you with him.

- Put your child to bed using the normal bedtime routine.

- Make sure your child has been to the lavatory and had a small evening drink. If you don't give him a drink, he might say he's thirsty, but if the drink is too big, he'll demand a trip to the lavatory. Cover yourself against such 'blackmail'!

- Say goodnight in the usual way and go out of the room.

- If your child says he needs a drink or the lavatory, stop yourself from answering these calls. Remember that he's already been to the lavatory and had a drink. If he comes out of his room to make these requests known again, tell him in a few short words that he's had them. And take him back to bed. (See Chapter 3)

- If he tells you he's wet the bed, consider ignoring him. You can clean this up later in the morning, if necessary.

Thousands of children wet the bed or their nappies every night and do not get cleaned up until morning. If this is a continual problem, put extra layers on the bed or in the nappy.

- If he starts head-banging, it may help to put him to bed on a mattress on the floor so he hasn't got a wall or headboard to bang against. Head-banging gives children a buzz especially if it gets your attention as well. Try to ignore it. There is little or no chance of it causing any lasting problems in children with normal development.

- Breath-holding? Ignore him. Children usually only do this with an audience. So don't give him one. Pretend it's an 'Empty House'.

  Children who hold their breath in temper will usually change colour and eventually faint and be unconscious for a short time. This always ends the breath-holding and your child will be back to normal in a few seconds.

  It is important to distinguish breath-holding from an epileptic fit. A fit occurs without any obvious cause, whereas breath-holding is associated with tempers or sudden distress. Consult your GP if you are not sure.

- Your child may scream himself sick. Remember how you caught him downstairs and marched him back without making a fuss. Don't give him any fuss when he's sick, either – even if it *has* ruined the carpet. Go in with two towels. Use one to wipe up the vomit and the other to put over the damp patch. *Don't* talk to your child or tell him what a bad boy he has been. And don't look your child in the face. Say your usual goodnight phrase and leave the room.

- Eventually, your child will fall asleep. It might take 10 minutes or it might take an hour or longer. But if you persevere with your side of the bargain – not to go in – *he* has to give in first by falling asleep with exhaustion.

If you stick to this plan, it always works. I have never known it take more than three nights to achieve a massive improvement.

But: If you start this approach and then give up half-way through, you may be worse off than before you started. If you go in to your child after he has been crying for an hour, for example, he may well continue crying for another hour tomorrow night because he knows you will come in eventually.

The 'in at the deep end' approach is rapid and effective, but if you panic and stop swimming, you may drown.

Warning!

The 'In at the deep end' approach to creating a good sleep habit has one particular risk.

If you start in a determined way and then give up half-way through, you could find that the problems are worse rather than better. If you change your mind about diving into the cold water you could do a belly flop! Imagine that you have left your child to cry for half an hour and then gone in because you couldn't stand it any longer. Not only will your child have been upset for no benefit but next night he will know to cry for at least 30 minutes because eventually he can win your attention.

If you think that there is a danger that you could give up half-way through the three-day programme then you should arrange extra support to cover this high risk time. Very few parents can manage the three-day programme entirely alone. Most people need a supportive spouse/friend/relative/health visitor/G.P. etc.

Make sure that you have got all the support that you need before you start *The New Baby and Toddler Sleep Programme.*

'I can't go through with this'

- You might well feel this on the first night. But by the second, it becomes easier. And by the third, you'll be surprised at how he'll begin to accept that even if he yells, you're not going to take him into the sitting room with you.

Remember that:

- As a parent, you have to set boundaries. Children actually like them – even if they don't follow them. If you allowed a child to do what he wanted, he'd feel lost eventually.

- Crying does not do babies and toddlers any harm if you have made sure that the only reason for crying is that they want to be with you. Your child probably cries and screams during the day. That doesn't do him any harm. So what is different about the night-time?

- Research shows that before the age of three, a child forgets what has happened to him. So he won't have any bad memories of being left to cry for a short time. How much can you remember clearly before you were three or even four years old?

- Remember that if your child is crying lustily, he must be very fit with lots of energy. If you are going to worry about your child, the most appropriate time to do this is when he stops crying and all is quiet. This is when you might want to turn the baby monitor on and listen for quiet, regular, breathing sounds.

'Yes, but it feels unkind to be so tough'

Hardening your heart to the sound of your child crying goes against all our instincts. So remind yourself why you're doing this. You're being tough to be kind. You're teaching your child to sleep well. You are giving him the following advantages:

- Teaching him to be secure with himself at night.
- Making sure he learns to stay safe in one place when you tell him.
- Helping him to feel more secure and self-confident during the day.
- Helping him to develop self-control.
- Helping him to concentrate better – something which happens after a good rest.
- Teaching him that when you say something, you mean it.
- Giving yourself time. This will make you a 'better' parent.

· *Billy* ·

Billy's parents had read that most babies sleep through the night before they reach the age of six months. But Billy was now six months old and there was no sign of him sleeping through the night. They decided to have him sleeping in a cot by their bed so that they could check that he was all right. They found that if Billy cried they could soon settle him down again with a cuddle or a feed. In fact, breastfeeding was so successful in stopping Billy from crying that his mother would use this method of calming him at any time of the day or night. The problem was that Billy's mum had had six months of sleep deprivation and was now feeling quite depressed and irritable and was rapidly running out of energy. The health visitor explained that Billy had been allowed to get into a routine that might suit him but certainly didn't suit his parents. Realising that it was better to change things sooner rather than later, Billy's parents decided that they would gradually move to a more regular feeding routine during the day and at night they would move him out of their bedroom and give him a dummy and a cuddly toy to keep him company. They were amazed to find that Billy soon started sleeping through the night and if he did cry he soon learnt to soothe himself back to sleep. When Billy was just over a year old he had a nasty cough and cold which woke him frequently during the night. Naturally, his parents went in several times during the night to comfort him and, when he recovered, Billy continued to cry and scream on and off during the night and would not stop until one or other parent went into the room. He would stop as soon as they lifted him out of the cot and then start crying and screaming again as soon as they put him back in. This went on for three weeks and there was no sign of it getting any better even though Billy was now quite fit and well. Billy's parents tried to follow the advice of the family doctor which was to leave him to scream but they found they were unable to do this because of the terrible sound that Billy made. Eventually, after much debate and heart-searching they decided that they would put Billy in the most sound-proof room in the house: the kitchen. The parents made absolutely certain that everything was safe and set up the baby alarm. They realised that if they kept the baby alarm on all the time there would be no point in having Billy in the kitchen so they only turned the baby alarm on when they wanted to check that Billy was all right and then they switched it off again. Billy's parents found it difficult to get off to sleep at first but they had a long cuddle and slept right through the night for the first time. They woke in a panic fearing that Billy might have come to some harm. They rushed to the kitchen and found him smiling and waving his toy around. They realised that Billy had moved on to another stage in his development towards independence.

It might help you to keep going if you remember that:

- If you don't, you might get stuck 'half-way' with a sleeping habit that's a compromise. It might be bearable and just liveable-with. But it won't be as effective as a good sleeping habit.

- If you can't be firm with your child about something that is quite safe, how will you cope in a dangerous situation? If you are not sure, you might as well practise being firm at bedtime. If you think you could cope with a dangerous situation, why not use the same approach and achieve the result you want with your child at night-time?

'I still can't cope. What should I do?'

- If you can cope with your child crying for three minutes, leave him to cry for that time.

- Then go in, show him you're there and go out again.

- Every evening, increase this by a minute or two minutes, etc. according to how much you can take.

Alternatively, you might feel strong enough to give the Three-Day Sleeping Plan another go.

The worst case scenario

It is important to prepare the ground for *The New Baby and Toddler Sleep Programme* by considering what could possibly go wrong. Hopefully the worst case scenario will never happen. But if it does you will be ready.

Wetting the bed in temper, head banging in temper, breath-holding in temper and vomiting in temper may all occur as a form of protest. The less attention you give to a protest, the less likely it is to occur again. We recommed the minimum intervention. You may feel that this is a bit hard. If you do, there is no reason why you shouldn't manage these problems differently. But remember – the more attention that you give the more likely the problems are to occur again.

The tough approaches recommended in *The New Baby and Toddler Sleep Programme* can only be justified in the context of a loving family – where parents are confident that their child is safe and well. And where parents are determined that the time has come to help their child onto the next rung of the ladder towards independence.

· *'I tried some of this but . . .'* ·

Here's another selection of common problems and how to deal with them:

'I'm worried that my child will hurt his lungs by crying'

This will not happen. In fact, he'll be showing you that his lungs are in perfect working order!

'Supposing he cries himself sick to get my attention?'

See page 92. If your child is sick, mop up the mess quietly without saying anything. Change your child if necessary but don't talk. Then go out of the room. The idea is to not to give him that attention he wants. Otherwise, he will be sick regularly as a habit.

'I don't like to see my child upset himself or get into an emotional trauma'

This is totally understandable. But there is no evidence that crying damages a child emotionally. Sooner or later, children are faced with a situation where they can't have what they want. It's better to tackle this in a safe, controlled environment. And it's best if *you* pick the time – such as bedtime.

Is crying harmful?

A crying baby is not the same as a crying grown-up. Crying is the only means of expression for a tiny baby. Toddlers and even older children use crying to get their demands met. But as children grow older they have to learn that crying has a powerful effect on other people and should only be used as a way of expressing emotions – either sadness and misery or happiness and joy.

Babies and toddlers quickly learn to use their crying

in a manipulative way. This is because crying has the power to control parents.

Nature has designed us to react quickly to a child's cries of distress. This is how it should be. However children sometimes use their crying to control and manipulate and this type of crying is best ignored.

To ignore the crying of a child who has good cause to be distressed could well be harmful. Indeed it could amount to a form of emotional abuse. To ignore the crying of a child who is demanding attention and being manipulative is quite justifiable. Indeed it may be harmful to respond to this type of crying as it will only make your child more likely to use crying as a way of getting his demands met.

· *Sarah* ·

Sarah was a delightful little girl of two but two or three times a day and often in the evening as well, she would have a terrible temper tantrum. The least little thing could start it off, although the tantrums occurred most commonly when she was asked to do something that she didn't actually want to do. There was no particular pattern to the tantrums and most of the time she would follow the bedtime routine quite happily. The tantrums were very severe. Sometimes she would bang her head. Other times she would hit out and kick anyone who happened to be near. Occasionally furniture got pushed over and damaged. When Sarah's parents discussed her behaviour with their friends, they realised that tantrums are very common at Sarah's age; this made them feel better but they still wondered what was the best way of coping. The most frequent advice they received was to ignore the tantrums. They tried doing this by carrying on as if nothing had happened, but this only seemed to make them worse. Eventually, they discovered that if they either turned their backs on her when she was having a tantrum, or walked out of the room if they knew she was quite safe, the tantrum would end more speedily. They also found that if they tried to move her somewhere else or pick her up, she usually got worse. The only other approach that worked was if she was held firmly until she had exhausted herself. This usually made the tantrum go on for much longer than it would have done otherwise. Although sometimes they had to hold her for almost half an hour, they did notice that after she had eventually calmed down, Sarah would then be much more self-controlled and calm in herself. The state of peace and tranquillity could last for several hours and occasionally even longer. Because the tantrums were so unpredictable, Sarah's parents weren't able to alter the routine in order to accommodate them and make them less likely to happen. However, they did find that Sarah soon calmed down if they left her to have her tantrum entirely on her own. They were then able to carry on with the bedtime routine, and by the time that Sarah was tucked up in bed, she had calmed down and was soon off to sleep.

There is also evidence that children exposed to carefully controlled stress situations show greater competence and resilience. If you over-protect them, they will be more vulnerable in later life.

All parents eventually have to teach their children that their crying demands will not be automatically and immediately met. Eventually, every parent reaches the point when it is just not possible to respond to the child's crying. It is better to do this during the first few years of life.

'I'm a soft-hearted person and I can't bear anyone to be upset'

It's a tough life out there. Children have to be self-confident and independent at an early age. However, if you can't cope, see page 97. You could also carry out a few jobs on the landing such as tidying the linen cupboard so that he knows you are around.

'I don't have enough energy to be firm and do what I know is best'

It's difficult, isn't it? But try to get more help and support from friends, relatives or from parent-support groups. Perhaps your GP or health visitor can help you.

'I feel guilty if I am tough on my child'

All parents feel guilty most of the time because parenting is impossible to get right all of the time. So don't worry too much. Do something nice with your child during the day to make up for the night before.

'I always start off with good intentions but then crack'

Try to work out in advance what makes you crack. Then plan ahead to avoid this problem next time. Is it because you are tired yourself and don't have the strength to continue? If so, try to go to bed earlier yourself. If necessary, get help for the critical moment. Ask your partner to come back early – it could only take three days to get this right, remember – or a friend to come over.

'I feel too fed-up and miserable to be bothered with any of this'

There is probably a good reason. Can you sort it out and deal with the cause of your misery? If not, it's wise to ask your family doctor for help.

'I am too busy'

That is a shame for your child. Parenting takes time. And developing good habits like sleeping will pay dividends in the end.

'I don't believe children should get upset'

That is a shame for you. There is no way of avoiding it so you are bound to be disappointed.

'I get my child to sleep by telling him I'm nearby. Then I do little jobs like ironing on the landing. Is this wrong?'

It's one way of dealing with it but it won't solve the problem. You'll soon have to tackle that crunch time when you've finished with the ironing and your child is still awake and doesn't want you to go away.

'I can only get my child to stay quietly in bed if I put him in the same bed or room as his brother'

That's not very fair on the sibling: it might well interfere with his own sleeping pattern and independence. And it could encourage the two of them to play instead of resting.

'I don't have enough bedrooms for my child to have one of his own. He has to share with his brother. How can I get them to sleep without playing?'

Be firm. Treat them as you would if they were in separate rooms. Tell them it's against the rules to talk. And if they start to get out of bed, do exactly what we've advised in previous chapters: take them back to bed with the minimum of talk or attention.

'My children have to share a bedroom. This makes it difficult to leave a child to cry'

Lots of children share bedrooms. It's not always something we have a choice about if space is limited.

So how can you put a sleep programme into action if your non-sleeping child is sharing a bedroom with a child who *wants* to sleep?

Or, even worse, how can you coax two non-sleepers to bed if one is jumping in and out of bed – and encouraging the other to do the same?

It's difficult. But it's by no means impossible.

Try:

- Sticking to your routine. Hang on to this word routine! It's worth its weight in gold!

- Pretending that each child is in a separate room. In other words, treat each one individually and do exactly the same as you would if he was in a room of his own.

But if this doesn't work:

- Divide and rule (again!). Put one child to bed in another place. Even if you haven't got a spare bedroom, there's always the sofa. Or granny's house. Or a friend's.

- Then follow the Three-Day Sleeping Plan outlined earlier in the chapter to get the non-sleeping child to rest. It is, after all, for only three days. Then the other child could come back to his own bed.

'I can only get my child to sleep if I put on a story tape. What's wrong with that?'

There will come a time when the tape will end. You might be lucky and find your child has drifted off. But if not, then what? Again, you're better off trying the deep-end approach without a tape. If you have to have one, fade out the tape every evening with shorter stories so your child eventually learns to go to sleep on his own.

> TIP: Rearrange your child's bedroom so it's a 'novelty' for him to go to sleep. A new duvet cover might make him want to climb into that bed.

Leaving your child to cry might sound tough, but it works. The 'softer', shallow-end methods mentioned above might feel better in the long term. But you could still be doing them long after your child goes to school.

Only you – and your partner – can decide what to do. But remember: nothing ventured, nothing gained! If you don't try it, you won't know how well it works.

> TIP: Keep a record to show what time you started the bedtime routine and what time your child eventually went to sleep.

CHAPTER FIVE

Waking in the night

Congratulations! You've done it. Your small reluctant sleeper has gone to bed. You've followed that bedtime routine to the letter. You've stopped him running down the stairs and you've persevered through that difficult 'Let-him-cry?' stage.

Your child's reward is that he's finally fallen asleep. If he stays asleep through the next night, he should wake up refreshed, alert and happy the next day. He won't feel grumpy or even over-active because he's over-tired and hasn't had enough rest. In other words, you'll have a nicer child in exactly the same way that you're likely to feel better about facing the world when you've had a good night's rest.

Your reward for all your efforts is that you actually have an evening to yourself. Remember what that word 'evening' used to mean in the days before children? A chance to unwind at the end of the day. An opportunity to talk to your partner about things which have nothing to do with children. Time to enjoy a meal, read a book or simply collapse in front of the television.

So far so good. You can do this now. Until, that is, your child decides to wake up in the night . . .

Don't panic. All is not lost. It doesn't mean that your child has won this sleeping battle after all. But what it does mean is that, just as you've got him to bed in the first place, you have to follow a set routine to get him back into it.

The trouble is that when your child wakes in the night, the chances are that you'll be asleep. We all vary as to how fast we become alert when someone wakes us up. Some of us take half an hour plus a cup of coffee to 'come to'. Others jump up immediately and then feel ghastly later. But most of us resent being woken up when we're not ready.

This leaves parents in a dangerously vulnerable frame of mind. We're tired. We don't want to spend half an hour coaxing our baby or toddler back to sleep. Why isn't our child asleep? Everyone else's child is . . .

Stop! Despite what other friends might tell you about their children sleeping through the night, it's not true of every child. Patterns change, too. A baby often learns to sleep for four or five hours at a trot before he's six months and then suddenly, at the age of two or so, he'll start to wake up for no apparent reason . . .

One good way of reassuring yourself that you are not the only one is to picture yourself looking down from the sky at a town or village. Look at all those lights which are on in the middle of the night. Peer through the windows and see all those parents trying to soothe a baby or child back to sleep.

The truth is that lots of children wake up during the night. Otherwise there wouldn't be a demand for a book like this. But if parents had more help in knowing what to do when their children woke, they'd be able to get them back to bed again. And this is exactly what we're going to do now.

· *Is it normal to wake during the night?* ·

The answer is 'yes'. Adults do it, too. We all sleep in cycles starting with a shallow cycle, then a deep cycle and then a shallow one, etc. The amount of time in each cycle depends on our age. Pre-school children usually go from shallow to deep and then to shallow within an hour. School-age children will take about one and a half hours. Adults usually sleep in two- to three- hour cycles.

A child will also naturally go through what is called REM sleep: Rapid Eye Movement. REM is also called active sleep because a lot of dreaming goes on. Information from daytime experiences is being sorted out and stored in long-term memory. Babies spend about 50 per cent of their sleeping time in REM sleep. They may make sucking movements, twitch a bit and smile. If the eyes are flickering open, you might mistakenly think your child is awake. If your child appears to be looking at you during that REM cycle, you might be tempted to talk to him, ask if he's all right and wake him up.

Your child may stir and move around when he returns to that shallow cycle. He may even cry, too. You have to learn to curb that natural tendency to go rushing in to see what's wrong.

Why? Because you too probably wake up in the night when you reach your shallow cycle, but over the years, you've learned to turn over and go back to deep sleep. Supposing, however, someone came in and patted you on the shoulder, asking if you're all right and offering a drink. Wouldn't that wake you up? Probably. The likelihood is that you'd then feel more reluctant to go back to sleep – especially if you hadn't really wanted to go to bed in the first place.

So it is for your child. Providing your child is both well and safe, he's more likely to go back to sleep on his own if you leave him to stir and even cry without going in.

· *What should I do if my child* · *wakes up crying?*

You have two main options. Either you can let him cry or you can go to see what is wrong. The first might sound tough. As usual, you should only let him cry if he is both well and safe. But here are the advantages of leaving a child over the age of six months to cry at night (six months is a reasonable age to start this because by this stage of development, most children should have a definite pattern of waking during the day and sleeping during the night):

Advantages of leaving your child to cry – if you know he is safe and well

- Because of the shallow/deep cycle, your child is likely to go back to sleep again when his body naturally takes him into the next stage, e.g., the deep cycle stage. He's learning a new trick in this amazing process of growing up. He's learning that although he might wake up, it's surprisingly easy to go back to sleep on his own. If you 'interfere' by going in and giving him a drink/talking to him/getting him up, you'll interfere with that natural cycle.

- If you go in and do any more than simply check your child is all right, you will soon create a waking habit for the baby. Even going into a toddler's bedroom during the night can start a waking habit if the child is aware that you are in the room.

- Most children quickly discover that they can control you by crying. There is nothing wrong with this because crying continues to be an important way of getting help. But children have to learn not to use this powerful way of communicating simply to manipulate people. Not responding to these crying demands for attention during the night will help your child to learn this important lesson.

- By not responding to your child's unreasonable demands for your undivided attention during the night, you are giving him a clear message that it is you who are in control and not him. Unfortunately, children who always have their demands met soon take control and become rather unlikeable – and it's only because you have allowed this to happen.

- Children who feel that their parents are in control of them, rather than the other way round, feel more secure.

· *Caroline* ·

Caroline was 18 months old and frequently cried during the night. Her parents had been told to leave her to cry and had tried this on several occasions. They found they could only listen to the crying for about five minutes before they decided it was too cruel to allow her to continue. They had been told by their parents that children who were left to cry later became emotionally disturbed. The longest they ever managed was 20 minutes and they felt really upset afterwards. Caroline also seemed to be distressed and cry even more. The parents felt very confused by the conflicting advice they had received so they asked their GP to refer them to the local child psychiatry clinic. They were told that by occasionally leaving Caroline to cry for a longer period and then on other occasions going in quite quickly they were actually encouraging her to cry because she knew that it was worthwhile crying for at least 20 minutes and she would be able to get her parents to come to her. The parents were also told that there was no evidence at all that leaving a child to cry could cause any emotional damage, provided that the child was safe and well and there were no obvious causes for the crying. Indeed, the research evidence tended to show that children benefited from coping with stressful events that were carefully managed and supervised by their parents. In spite of this reassurance, Caroline's parents still felt uncomfortable about leaving her to cry. They decided that they would take the slow approach and allow Caroline to cry for one more minute on each occasion before going in to her. This seemed to work well at first but they soon found they were allowing Caroline to cry for 20 minutes before they went in and they seemed to be making very little progress. In fact, she seemed to be getting worse rather than better. It was all getting so difficult that they decided to give it a break for a few weeks and then start again. Next time round it was a bit easier but it wasn't long before Caroline was again crying for long periods. It was at this point that her father decided that enough was enough and with his wife's agreement he decided to take control and allow Caroline to cry for as long as she wished. Caroline's mother found this extremely difficult to cope with. She found the first night so distressing that she decided to use ear plugs. When she awoke the next morning, she was surprised to hear that Caroline had slept right through the night and was delighted when this happy state of affairs continued.

Still worried?

- You can always listen in on the monitor or hover outside to check he's all right. But don't let him realise you're there or your cover will be blown!

Parenthood isn't easy. Sometimes you have to be tough to be kind. It's hard work wrapping up that present for your child's future when the paper doesn't want to fold neatly. But if you persevere, you'll make the present look wonderful. You'll be giving yourself and your child a good sleep habit. And you'll both enjoy each other's company more the next day because neither of you will be so tetchy.

· *Being your child's 'dummy'* ·

Your toddler is crying. Does he want a drink? Does he want a cuddle? What could be more natural?

Again, that's fine if that's what you want. But remember that if you go in, tuck him up and give him a drink, he'll be more likely to wake during that shallow, vulnerable phase. Then he'll need your presence to get him back to sleep.

In other words, you'll soon become his comforter. Or, to put it another way, you'll be his dummy! You might not mind that at the moment. You may even find it comforting yourself to know that your child is awake and needs you. Parenthood is a scary business, especially when it's dark and fears get out of proportion. We look after our children all day and then at night, we expect them to manage on their own for the night. And the truth is that they can.

If you don't mind being your child's dummy, that's up to you. But do you really want to carry on being that dummy when he's five, six, seven or even eight years old? At some point, he has to learn to go back to sleep on his own. It's an important step in that ladder of self-dependence. And the sooner you give him a leg-up onto that ladder, the steadier he'll be when he gets onto the second rung.

Did you know?

Research shows that the more a parent tries to make a child go to sleep, the less likely it is that the child will sleep through the night. The less interference, the better.

'I can't bear to hear him crying in the night'

Of course you can't. As we've said before, we're conditioned to respond when a child cries. But remember, waking is normal. And so is going back to sleep naturally. It's been proved with video cameras when both sleeping children and adults are filmed. They wake up, move around and open their eyes during that shallow cycle and then go back to sleep again.

Picture your child having a meal. He's sitting up at a table eating a plate of nutritious food which you've lovingly prepared for him. You wouldn't snatch that away from him, would you? Similarly, you shouldn't 'snatch' his sleep away from him by disturbing him when he's naturally sleeping lightly anyway. You'll be taking away all that goodness which sleep and rest can bring.

Remember, too, that even if your child cries during that shallow phase, it doesn't necessarily mean he's upset. Babies and even toddlers often find crying comforting. It's familiar. It's almost like talking to themselves. You probably make little noises yourself during the night.

Of course, some cries aren't like that. But by now, you'll be able to recognise the kind of cry your child is making from its sound . . . You'll know from experience whether it's a 'Help, something awful is happening' cry or a tired cry which will soon peter out.

If your child has worked himself up and is really yelling but you know he is well and safe, you can comfort yourself by realising that if he's crying that loudly, there can't be anything wrong with his lungs or energy levels. Perhaps he's going to be a good singer one day . . .

Remember that all children will soothe themselves sooner or later. But you must always make sure that they are safe and well before you leave them to cry.

Did you know?

It's worth using a soother because:

Babies can be divided into self-soothers and non-self-soothers. Those who soothe themselves, wake and go quietly off to sleep again. Self-soothers are more likely to use a cuddly toy, a comforter like a blanket, a thumb or a dummy. Non-self-soothers wake and cry out. They are more likely to depend on their parents to quieten them.

'How old should my baby be before I let him cry himself back to sleep?'

As a rough guide, you should always consider going in to a crying baby under six months. But between six months and a year, you'll see that he sleeps longer between the hours of midnight and 5 a.m. than he used to. A clear pattern of day-time waking and night-time sleeping will also have been formed.

This is when you need to start getting into the habit of helping him to help himself to go back to sleep.

Also, by this time, you will have got to know your child and be able to work out the difference between a genuine cry for help and attention-seeking when there is nothing wrong.

Obviously this isn't going to happen overnight. So play it

by ear. But remember that the sooner you start, the more effective it will be.

'Supposing my child is hungry?'

From six months onwards, your child's body should have automatically conditioned itself to cope without food for five or six hours during the night. If, however, you offer a bottle or a drink, he'll assume you will do this every time he wakes up. And he'll get into the habit of wanting a nightcap! If you continue to feed him during the night, there is also a risk that he will put on too much weight.

'Supposing my child is thirsty?'

The same applies to a toddler. If you ignore his cries for a drink, you're not being cruel. He won't die of thirst or hunger by not having a drink for a few hours. Think of it this way: occasionally we all wake in the night feeling peckish, especially if we didn't eat dinner the night before. But if we then turn over and go back to sleep, it's not going to hurt us. All that will happen is that we will be more likely to want breakfast in the morning.

Alternatively, you could leave a small beaker of water next to his bed so that he can help himself. But make sure it is water. Anything tastier – such as milk or fruit juice – will make him realise it's worth his while to wake up and he will soon get into the waking habit. Fruit juice on tap through the night is also bad for his teeth.

'I can't leave him to cry but my partner says I should'

You could ask your partner to take over responsibility for the crying child and for comforting you when your child cries. Maybe she/he doesn't realise how much it is affecting you – especially if you tend to be the waking partner.

It's a sad fact that some marriages hit the rocks after the birth of a child. Especially if you disagree on how the child should be brought up. (See also Chapter 11: Time for you).

A crying child produces very strong emotions in parents and it is all too easy for arguments to develop when you in an emotional state.

There aren't any easy solutions. Apart, that is, from the obvious one of talking about it. Discuss sleeping just as you would discuss other areas like eating, learning to walk and learning to talk. Listen to each other's views. You might learn something yourself if you're not too convinced that only you are right. And try to reach a compromise.

If you can't, why not try it his or her way, first? If that doesn't work, do a swap. Try the other method. But don't let your child's sleeping problems creep into your bedroom life, too.

Why not read this book together and support each other in following the guidelines? If you follow them carefully, you will find they work.

'It's easier to take him into our bed'

You're tired. It's the middle of the night. You need your sleep too. It's so much easier to take him into your bed.

There are two ways of looking at this.

- You're becoming his comforter once more, aren't you? And although that might not matter in the dark of the night when you're desperate for sleep, it won't help him to become independent and develop a good sleep habit in the long run.

- It might stop *you* from sleeping. If your child is still a baby, you probably won't sleep well in the fear that you might roll over and hurt him. If he's a toddler, the chances are that he'll wriggle. By the time morning comes, you will wake up feeling as though you haven't had a wink of sleep.

Think of it this way. If you're short of cash, you could take control of your finances or you could borrow money. This would make you feel better for a short time. But the more you borrow, the more interest you have to pay back. The longer it goes on, the worse it gets.

It's the same with sleeping habits. The more you look for quick and easy solutions by 'borrowing' peace and quiet, the harder it is going to be in the long run.

'It feels unkind to leave him in his bed, crying'

Then try this 'shallow-end', alternative approach. Stand at your child's door without saying anything or sit quietly by his bed, out of reach. He can see you there. He knows you're around. But he also knows that you're not going to start the day in the middle of the night in the way he wants. After a few minutes, go back to your own bed. On each occasion, reduce the amount of time you are there.

But . . .

The trouble with this is that even a small glimpse of you may make him worse. If he yells again, you could come back. Will you? That's up to you. But remember that quick and easy solutions often have a high cost in the long term.

'My husband or I have to work in the morning. If we leave our child to cry, we'll be too tired to cope'

Then re-think everyone's sleeping places. Perhaps the working partner should consider moving to the spare bedroom or sofa for a few nights. It won't be for long – just until your child learns that he can go back to sleep on his own. Alternatively, move your child so his cries aren't so loud.

But remember. Wherever your child is, he must be safe.

'I can't stand the noise'

Buy a pair of ear plugs. Your child will probably then stop screaming sooner than you think. It's amazing how 60 seconds of yelling can seem more like 60 minutes when it's on full volume!

· *Wandering around out of bed* ·

Waking up in the night is one thing. But getting out of bed is a different ball game. So you need to look again at the rule book – fast. It is important that you and your partner agree on the rules. During the day, you're probably watching your toddler most of the time. We all know that they're capable of doing some pretty terrible things within seconds. If you weren't looking, goodness knows what could happen . . .

If your toddler or older child wakes up at night and starts wandering round the house when you are asleep, it could be very dangerous.

If you are worried about your child's safety, make sure:

- There's a stairgate on your child's bedroom door – and he's not able to climb over it.

- The house is safe. Has anyone left pill bottles/razors/medicines within reach?

- There are no electric or gas points that he could interfere with.

- There aren't any fires or anything very hot to harm him.

- He can't get through any windows or doors.

· *Build your own house alarm kit!* ·

It's important – for safety reasons – to know when your toddler is wandering around at night especially if you are a deep sleeper and unlikely to hear him coming out of his room.

Here are some tips on how to know when this is happening:

- Fix an alarm system on his door so you know if he comes through it. Either buy one from a DIY shop or make your own by hanging a little bell on the knob or even the door so that it is knocked when the door is opened.

- An even cheaper method is to tie a clutch of saucepans to the child's bedroom door and put them on a chair. When the door opens, the pans will fall onto the floor making a terrible din!

- Keep your baby monitor on – but resist the temptation to go rushing in if you hear the usual 'shallow cycle' waking noises on it.

TIP: As soon as you have got to know your baby it is a good idea to leave the monitor off and only put it on when you want to check that all is well. Otherwise you may become 'hooked' on listening to it. You can't listen to it for 24 hours a day.

· *Peter* ·

Peter was a very determined boy and now that he was four years old, his parents found it particularly difficult to divert him away from anything that he had decided to do. Unfortunately, Peter had decided that he didn't want to sleep in his bedroom. He preferred to sleep in his parents' bedroom. Preferably in their bed, between them. Peter's parents knew about the importance of being firm and setting clear limits. However, in Peter's case this seemed only to make matters worse and what started off as quite a simple disagreement soon got out of hand, with Peter sulking and trying to do what he wanted anyway. Whatever the parents tried, however firm they were and however determined, Peter always seemed to end up in their bed. His father became so fed-up with this and so determined not to be beaten by a little four-year-old, that he decided he would stay quietly outside Peter's bedroom door and return him to bed every time he tried to come out. Peter behaved rather like a 'Jack-in-the-Box' for the rest of the evening and was still coming out at midnight, although it wasn't as frequent as earlier in the evening. At this point Peter's father decided that he was going to sleep outside Peter's bedroom in order to make sure that Peter knew that it was the parents in control and not him. In the end, Peter's father slept outside the bedroom door for a week, although Peter got the message after four nights.

'What do I do if my child starts wandering around the house?'

Remember when you put him to bed and he kept coming down to see what you were up to? You didn't talk to him. You simply walked him in front of you back to his room. Your expression was serious. And you used key words like 'Back to bed' (see pages 62–5).

Now you do exactly the same, even if your brain is only half-working because you're half-asleep. Escort him back to bed and say your magic goodnight phrase firmly but kindly: 'Good night, sleep tight'. If he gets out of bed, do the same thing again, and again . . . Don't allow this to be repeated too many times.

'But he needs the lavatory'

If your toddler isn't potty trained and he's damp, use extra wadding the next night. Change your nappy brand. Or put an extra liner in. Research shows that toddlers don't usually wake because they are wet. In fact, they usually wet just as they are waking up anyway.

Keep a spare set of clean nightwear handy so you don't wake him up even more by turning on the lights to look for clean clothes. Change him if necessary without speaking. This is no time for a natter . . . The reason for this is that the more he wakes up, the more likely it is that this will become part of his sleep habit.

If your child is potty-trained and wants the lavatory, that's fair enough. But only once. If he keeps needing it, it's probably an excuse. But to make sure, take him to the doctor. Perhaps he has a urinary problem. (See also pages 130–2.)

'He's got a tummy ache'

Is it an excuse or does he mean it? If he's really ill, you'll soon know. If it's a tummy ache every night, he's either having you on or he needs to visit the GP.

'He's scared of the dark'

If he's always been used to dark rooms, this won't happen. But, if not, try a dim bulb or a dimmer switch. Gradually fade it out as the days and weeks go by. Traditionally, we're taught to be scared of the dark. But you can teach children that it's comforting, too. The more you feed the fear – by leaving the light on – the worse it gets. Keeping the light on gives your child the frightening message that darkness is dangerous and must be banished with the help of lights. As we know, that's not true . . .

'There's a monster in his room!'

Of course there isn't! Look under the bed – see. There's nothing there! The problem is that if you look under the bed or draw back the curtains to show nothing is hiding, you're perpetuating the myth that there might be something there in the first place. You're accepting that there might be something there because you're having to prove there isn't!

Instead, simply say, 'Things like that don't exist' or words to that effect. And be careful what your child watches on video or television.

It is now proved that what children watch can have a bad effect on them and can make some children very anxious. Fears of monsters and darkness are most frequent between the ages of four and six and affect as many as 80 per cent of children.

'We only have one bedroom so our child has to share our room'

This isn't easy but try to follow the same rules. If your child cries, don't get up. Try to stick it out. Take him back if he gets out. Perhaps you could create a partition by hanging a curtain across the room so his bed/cot is on one side and your bed is on the other. If he doesn't see you, you might find it's easier for him to go back to sleep.

'My child gets into my bed but I don't notice until I wake up'

This sounds more like your problem than his! Perhaps you should watch out – if he can get in, undetected, so might anyone. Perhaps it's time to buy a burglar alarm . . . Remember too that adult beds can be dangerous for children. They weren't designed with children in mind. And it is possible for your child to fall out or get squashed.

'He climbs into the other children's beds'

This might sound like a good idea – especially if it lets you sleep. But it's not fair on brothers and sisters, is it? They need a good night's rest too. And they won't get it if they're woken up by a small, fidgety toddler.

'I can't stop checking my child in the night'

The irony is that when your little one does eventually begin to sleep for a decent stretch of time, you will have trained your body to be alert for his nocturnal movements.

So even though he may be sleeping soundly, you may be waking up and wondering if he's all right . . .

Such fears are totally understandable. You have your child next to you all day. Now you're apart for 10 to 12 hours. What could be more natural than getting up in the night 'just to check' on him?

The problem is that if you do that, you might wake him – especially if he's going through that shallow stage of the sleeping cycle. And then you'll be back to where you started.

Try to be rational. If your child weren't all right, he'd probably be yelling. Of course it is natural to check on small babies regularly, but as your child grows up, you will become more confident in knowing when he is quite well and strong and able to manage without you. Most parents know their toddlers well enough to leave them to sleep through the night without checking – apart from at bedtime.

> TIP: Keep a torch by your bedside. Then, if you hear your child wandering around in the night, you have a light to guide him back to bed. This is better than turning on a main room switch so the brightness wakes him up even more.

> TIP: Talk to him in whispers. It will reinforce the idea that night is for resting/sleeping and not playing. And it will calm you down so you're not tempted to say loudly, 'Why are you out of bed?' If you are calm, he's more likely to be calm and more willing to go back to where he was before.

> TIP: You can tell which parent is the soft, indulgent one because if your child comes into your bedroom during the night, he will always go to the 'soft' parent, even if this means walking right round the bed. And if he gets into bed, he will get in on the side of the softer parent.

If you find it hard to take your child back to bed but your partner thinks you *should*, try swopping sides. Your child will probably be used to coming to 'your' side of the bed for sympathy. If he comes to the 'wrong' side, your partner could take him back. If your partner doesn't want to be disturbed because he or she is going to work the next day, save this method for weekends.

CHAPTER SIX

Nocturnal problems

Some people find the darkness soothing; others find that it exaggerates fears they may have during the day. How will I tackle that business meeting tomorrow? How will I get everything done at home?

It has a similar effect on our attitude to parenting. Being a mother or father can be great fun. But it's also scary. We have a responsibility to bring up our children safely. And no one has really shown us how to do it. It's like starting a new job without a manual.

The dark can make these fears even worse, especially if you haven't learned to relax when your child is asleep in one room and you're in bed in another. All sorts of worries might come crowding into your mind: 'Is my daughter ill – after all, she *was* a bit warm when I put her to bed?' Or, 'What was that noise? Could my son be choking?'

Here's a list of some common night-time behaviour patterns together with some practical advice on what to do. Many of them are perfectly normal. But it's useful to be aware of them.

Nightmares These usually occur in the last two-thirds of the night, normally just before waking. They happen most commonly as part of a developmental phase between the ages of two and teenage years. Around 50 per cent of five-year-olds have nightmares, although they decrease with age and are usually a passing phase.

Nightmares occur more often if a child is anxious or stressed. They can also be caused by a traumatic event, a frightening television/video programme or some medicines.

Most nightmares have no obvious cause and have no special significance. However, if the same nightmare recurs night after night, it may have a meaning for the child.

· *Rachel* ·

Rachel was six years old when she was involved in a road traffic accident. The car in which she was travelling was hit by another car that crashed into them from behind when the brakes failed. Rachel's father, who was driving, had to be taken to hospital for severe bruising and Rachel was examined in the Accident and Emergency Department before she was allowed to go home. For the next six weeks she slept badly and most nights would wake screaming after a nightmare. The nightmare was almost exactly the same on each occasion and was about the accident. During the day she was less lively than normal and her appetite was poor. She became much more tense and anxious and repeatedly talked about the accident and how it had happened. Rachel's parents consulted their GP who explained that Rachel had typical symptoms of Post Traumatic Stress Disorder in which poor sleep and nightmares about the traumatic event are common features. The symptoms normally fade away after four to six weeks and fortunately this is what happened for Rachel. She continued to have an occasional nightmare about the accident and was anxious when travelling by car but this gradually improved over the next year.

What to do:

- Go in and reassure your child with the 'magic' bedtime phrase. Reassure him it's all right. Gently tuck him in and leave the room as soon as you can.

- Keep a chart. Is your child having nightmares for a particular reason? Is he worried about playschool or another child? Is there any pattern to the nightmares?

- Repeated nightmares can often be controlled. For example, if the dream involves a monster chasing your child, work out a plan with your little one to deal with the monster. You could do this while he's still in bed. For example, you could suggest to your child that you could both make this monster fall into a hole, drown or get trapped in a cage.

This plan works because nightmares occur in the lighter stages of sleep which makes dreams more easy to control. A child's imagination is also more adaptable than an adult's and open to suggestions.

Did you know?

Around 50 per cent of five-year-olds have nightmares. They decrease with age and are usually a passing phase.

In the morning, ask older children if they want to tell you about it. Talking about nightmares can sometimes help. But if you dwell on them too much, it might also increase the likelihood of repetition.

Night terrors   These are different from nightmares. For a start, they occur in the deepest part of the sleep: in other words, during the first third of the night. Your child will be very agitated and probably move around the cot or bed. He'll appear to be awake but won't be. He'll also seem very frightened with rapid breathing and a fast heart rate. His eyes will appear to be staring at you. It can be scary. What is wrong with your child?

The answer is: nothing. The experience is probably more frightening for you than for him because he doesn't really know what he is doing. Research shows that children never remember night terrors in the morning.

What to do:

- Don't try to wake him up. It's almost impossible and will upset you and him even more.

- Wait patiently next to him. The terror will soon pass. It usually only lasts a few minutes, although it could go up to half an hour.

- As soon as he has quietened down, tuck him in quietly and say that familiar bedtime phrase to reassure him.

- Keep a chart. If the terrors are happening regularly, wake him up just before they're about to start so you interrupt the sleep cycle. Then coax him back to sleep again. If it continues, see your GP.

- We've already said that your child won't remember his night terror in the morning. So don't get too worried – it is usually a passing phase.

· *Ben* ·

Ben was five years old when he started waking at about 11 o' clock at night. His parents would be startled by a blood-curdling yell. They would rush in to see what had happened to Ben and there he would be, sitting up in bed looking scared out of his wits with wide-open staring eyes, waving his arms around as if to fight off a monster. Ben's parents tried to calm him down but whatever they did seemed either to make things worse or have no effect at all. After consulting their GP, who told them that Ben was having night terrors, his parents learnt to stay calm with Ben during the night terror and simply protect him from coming to any harm. They were told that if they tried to wake Ben up he would be completely confused and disorientated and it was better to wait until the terror passed and then simply tuck him up in bed and leave the room. It was amazing how Ben was completely unaware of what had happened during the night when his parents asked him about what had happened. Fortunately the phase passed in a few months and Ben only had 10 night terrors in all. His school work and his general development were unaffected.

Did you know?

Night terrors are more common in boys. They also run in families.

Sleepwalking Like night terrors, this occurs in the first third of the night when your child is in a deep sleep. It also tends to run in families.

What to do:

1. Do not try to wake your child. Lead him gently back to bed and make sure he settles. Tuck him in and say the magic words.

2. Check there aren't any obstacles for him to fall over. Lock windows and doors. Keeping your child safe is the most important thing you can do. This is usually only a passing phase.

3. If it happens regularly, make a chart and see if there's any particular reason or pattern behind it.

4. Sometimes it can be difficult to tell if a child is truly sleepwalking or awake and wandering about. Sleepwalkers only do rather simple things. If the child is carrying out a complex series of actions he is very unlikely to be sleepwalking.

Did you know?

One in six children sleepwalk at some stage, usually as they approach adolescence.

Snoring Ten per cent of children snore regularly. It may be a symptom of Obstructive Sleep Apnoeia. Although this is a rather rare condition, it is important to recognise it because it causes problems for the child during the daytime.

Obstructive sleep apnoeia   Common symptoms include:
- Snoring
- Breath-holding while asleep
- Restlessness
- Mouth breathing
- Sleepiness during the day
- Difficult, irritable behaviour
- Hyperactivity

It might be caused by:

- Airway obstruction, e.g., tonsils and adenoids
- Obesity
- Blocked nose
- Parental smoking

What to do:

See your GP.

Did you know?

Twelve per cent of children snore between the ages of four and seven. If they do snore, they are also more likely to sleep during the day, be hyperactive or/and be restless sleepers. Most children grow out of snoring but some children start between the ages of four and seven. Snoring also usually decreases with age. So if your child is snoring at five, he'll probably stop by seven. If you're worried, see your GP.

Sleep-talking

What to do:

Nothing! Sleep-talking is perfectly natural. You might even learn a thing or two about your child's private life! However, most sleep-talking is just mumbo jumbo.

Don't try to wake your child. If he is agitated, smooth his brow, say that magic bedtime phrase and help him to turn over and go back to sleep.

Sleep-talking usually occurs in deep sleep and is not remembered.

Night-time coughing and snuffles This is miserable for both you and your child. You've managed to get him to sleep but you can't sleep well yourself because the cough is making him restless.

What to do:

- Check his room isn't too damp or dry. Nor should it be too hot or too cold.
- If he's coughing more when he's lying down, it could be due to large tonsils or what is known as a 'post nasal drip'. This occurs when catarrh empties out of the sinuses and trickles down the back of the throat. If the throat is irritated or there are large tonsils, this can cause coughing – especially when the child is lying down.
- Try simple remedies such as:
  1. Helping him to sit up. Also try raising the top end of the bed by putting bricks or books underneath.

     If your child is old enough to have a pillow, give him an extra one so you are raising his chest.
  2. Giving him a small sip of water or honey drink to soothe the throat.
  3. Giving him a steam inhalation. For younger children, close the windows and doors and put on a kettle without a lid. When it boils, the steam should fill the room so they breathe it in.

     For an older child, you could fill a basin with boiling water and help him to hold his head about it – never touching – with a towel over his head so he inhales steam. Make sure it is not too hot for him.

4. Be wary of cough medicines. Most contain drugs that can make children restless and irritable. There is no real evidence that any cough medicine is better than honey, water or any other simple remedy.

   Or you could try vapour decongestants which your child can breathe in instead of swallowing, such as Carvol. You could also buy a plug-in vapouriser from the chemist.

Coughing is not serious if your child:

- Is well in other respects.
- Is eating well.
- Is normally active.
- Is breathing normally.

If in doubt, consult your GP.

Teeth grinding (also known as bruxism) This is more common in older children and is worse in times of stress. It may sound odd but it doesn't have any special significance.

What to do:

Simply changing the pillows may be enough to stop this particular bedtime habit. If necessary, alter the position of the bed. Sometimes, changes like this can produce changes in sleeping habits.

It may also be worth visiting the dentist. Continual teeth grinding could cause dental problems, and a special tooth protector may be necessary.

Bed-wetting This isn't usually considered a problem until the child is five. Don't feel you're the only one who has a child with this problem. Ten per cent of all five-year-olds wet their beds at night. It's also more common in boys – and it runs in families.

Bed-wetting is caused by:

- Developmental delay/immaturity.
- Bladder infections (rarely).
- Lack of training or delayed training.

It's made worse by:

- Stress of any kind, including excitement.

What to do:
- Make a reward chart with stickers for dry nights (For more ideas, see the section on Rewards in Chapter 7.)

- See your GP who might prescribe drugs which can help your child if he has to sleep away from home. However, all medicines only stop the symptoms and do not help bladder control to mature.

- Your GP might also prescribe an 'enuretic alarm'. This is a battery-operated gadget which buzzes when the child is wet. It works on the principle that urine conducts electricity. There are two main types of alarm: in one, a low-voltage electric current is conducted between two metal and gauze pads placed under the bed sheets. In the other type of alarm, the current passes between contacts on a small electrode hidden in a pad in your child's pants.
  The theory is that your child wakes with the noise when he starts to 'wee' and can then be trained to go to the lavatory. Eventually, he will learn to do so without the bell. The method has been found to be successful in 80 per cent of cases.

- Reduce the amount of drink your toddler has before going to bed. Explain why you are doing this. It probably won't stop the wetting but it will reduce the amount of urine passed.

- Avoid drinks like cola and tea or coffee containing caffeine which stimulate the production of urine.

- Lift your toddler out of bed to take him to the lavatory before you go to sleep. *But* this could interfere with his sleeping cycle and wake him up! And it does not train your child. He may leave the responsibility for his bladder control to you.

- Try the Dry Bed Method in conjunction with an enuretic alarm. This has been shown to have a 90 per cent success rate in six weeks. But it's not easy!

It works like this:

Help your child to practise getting out of bed and going to the lavatory 20 times. Before he does this, he has to count up to 20 in bed and then another 20 in the lavatory. On the first night wake your child every hour, give him a drink and ask if he wishes to go to the lavatory. If he does, you should praise him. But if he has an accident and wets the bed, the 20 times routine has to be repeated and the child helps the parent to change the sheets – or does it on his own . . .

During future nights, encourage your child to drink normally. But when the buzzer sounds, indicating that he's wet the bed, the child should go to the lavatory and then change the sheets. If the child has wet the bed the night before, he has to repeat the 20 times routine before going to bed at night. If he has been dry there is no need to do the 20 times routine.

Keep a record, and if your child is dry for seven nights, remove the buzzer. But if the child wets himself for two consecutive nights, return the buzzer. This intensive training method works by a technique called overlearning.

Colic   It's easy to mistake ordinary crying for colic. So, if you interfere *too* much, it can encourage your child to wake again and again.

In fact, colic is normal between the ages of three to four months and only becomes a problem in about 15 per cent of children. Even then, no real explanation has ever been found for its occurrence. It's possible that crying itself may cause air to be trapped in the stomach, causing pain.

What to do:

- Simple remedies are best, such as a soother (dummy or comfort blanket or cuddly toy). Remember, it will pass.
- Check that there isn't another cause for pain, such as nappy rash/thrush/earache. If in doubt, see your GP.

· *Claire* ·

Claire was three months old when her parents became concerned that her crying was so extreme that she must have colic. They consulted their GP who told them that excessive crying is common during the first three to six months. The crying usually occurs on more than three days a week and totals more than three hours a day. The infant seems to be in pain and does not respond to soothing. The GP went on to explain that no one is really sure about the cause of colic and it tends to improve with time. It is thought that a small minority of babies with colic have a reaction against cows' milk. Occasionally changing the way a baby is fed can improve the crying. The most common cause for persistent crying in the first six months of life is simply normal growing up as babies learn what effect they have on the world around them. Claire's parents were reassured by this explanation and found it easier to cope with the crying as they knew there were only another two or three months left before they could expect the crying to improve on its own.

Thumb-sucking About 20 per cent of children under five years suck their thumbs. Research also shows that thumb-suckers are more likely to use a soother later on like a blanket, cuddly toy or dummy.

Obviously, there are pros and cons. On the plus side, a thumb-sucker is less likely to wake at night; he's got his thumb to look after him!

On the minus side, the longer thumb-sucking continues, the more difficult it will be to 'kick' the habit. Some children continue sucking their thumbs until they're 10, 11, 12 or even into their teens.

Thumb-sucking after the age of three to four may alter the way the mouth, jaws and teeth grow. And thumb-sucking during the day may interfere with communication and cause the child to be teased. The best way of dealing with it is to think of ways to keep the thumb busy, away from the mouth. Maybe you could encourage an older child to take up knitting! Another 'trick' is to get the child to hold his thumb in the palm of his hand.

Sleeping positions Some children end up in the most peculiar positions when they're asleep! If you're worried, you could try to straighten them without waking them, but it might be your child's way of saying he's comfortable. Just as you can only sleep on the right-hand side of the bed with one pillow . . .

If they tend to throw the bed clothes off and wake up cold and shivering, invest in an all-in-one sleep suit and if necessary an extra jumper. Layers can be very useful in winter (vest, T-shirt, sweatshirt). But don't overheat a baby or young toddler.

· *Cot death* ·

Many parents are tempted to check their babies and toddlers at night because they're scared of cot death. It's a fear which many parents share so don't think you're being silly.

You can, however, stop yourself from worrying so much if you know you've done everything possible to prevent it – such as:

- Breastfeeding your baby. Studies show that this reduces the risk of cot death.

- Putting your baby to sleep on his back. The latest research shows that this is the best position. If he's on his front, it might interfere with his breathing.

- Making sure your baby/younger toddler isn't too hot. Feel his skin. Is he wearing too much? Is the room very warm? As a guideline, it should feel 'comfortable' to you without being either too hot or cold.

- Not smoking – the same goes for your partner.

- Keeping babies in the same room as you for the first three to six months. Although there is no evidence that this makes cot death less likely, it will help you to know what is happening to your child and whether he is ill or not.

Still worried? It's not easy, is it? But remember there are some things which are outside our control such as:

- Infection
- Your child's immunity system not working efficiently
- Prematurity.

If you are concerned about any of the above, see your doctor for advice. If there is a history of cot death in your family, you should also consult your doctor.

However, try not to worry too much. Parenthood *can* be a scary business. But it should also be enjoyable. Concentrate on the fun you have with your child. Don't dwell on the things which might go wrong.

CHAPTER SEVEN

Good morning!

You might wonder why we need a chapter on morning. After all, this is a book about getting your child to sleep. By morning time, it's too late.

The fact is that morning is a good time to reflect on how you got your child to bed the night before and where you went wrong – or right.

Sometimes it helps to make a list. Use the checklist at the beginning of the book to aid you. What helped to get your child to sleep eventually? What didn't help? Can you do the same things again?

· *It isn't morning yet!* ·

Parents often complain that they manage to get their children to sleep for most of the night. But their children are then up too early, such as 5 or 6 a.m. One mother constantly complained that she was exhausted having to start her day at the crack of dawn.

What to do:

- Set a definite time for getting up.
- Pretend it's 1 or 2 a.m. – even if it's later. Do exactly what you would do in the middle of the night. If your child is wandering around the house or hovering by your bed, take him back to bed. Use simple words and a firm voice. If your child is still in his cot, do what you would do in the middle of the night. Leave him to settle. Let him learn the rest by himself.

You could, of course, go in, show your face to reassure him. But, as in the earlier chapters, you're more likely to make him yell because he wants to see your face again . . .

> TIP: Buy your child his own alarm clock or lend him one. He's only allowed to get out of bed when that alarm goes. Even toddlers can understand this. Make it a special 'present'. Say: 'Aren't you grown-up? You even have your own alarm now.'

· *Time to get up!* ·

Children are dab hands at moving the goal posts. Last night, they wouldn't go to bed. Now they don't want to get up in the morning . . .

If your children are still at home all day, that might not matter too much. But sooner or later, one will need to be at school by a certain time. And then, you'll need to get yourself into a routine. So why not start now?

Thirty per cent of school-age children need to be woken for school in the morning. And if they need to be woken, they might not be very alert for lessons because they are not getting enough sleep.

Try:

- Organising a definite getting-up routine for the morning and sticking to it in the same way as the bedtime routine.

- Bringing the bedtime routine forward by one hour or half an hour. If they go to bed earlier, they might get to sleep earlier and then wake up when you want them to.

- Giving your children time to wake up. Children are like adults. Some are natural early-birds. Others take time to get used to the waking world. If you let your child lie in until the last possible moment, there'll be a horrible rush before nursery/school/anything else you may have planned. Rushing invariably means a bad-tempered child, not to mention a bad-tempered adult. Is it worth it?

TIP: Start to wake your child up gently at least 15 minutes before you really need him to get up. Turn on a radio on the landing or sing as you get his clothes out. It will give him time to 'come to'.

· *Rewards* ·

Morning is also the time when you can praise your child for being so good during the night. When your child has done what you've asked, you can reward him for being good. It's an incentive for doing it again. If someone gave you a bottle of wine/salary rise every time you cleaned the house well or wrote a good office report, you'd try to do the same again, wouldn't you? Even if your child has not stayed in bed and been quiet all night, it is important to find something that you can praise and reward, such as 'Well done, you were up one less time than the previous night'.

What kinds of reward?

- **Cuddles** A simple cuddle or special one-to-one attention is often just as nice as a new toy or bar of chocolate. Sometimes, in our materialistic society, we forget that this is more important than anything. And it only costs time.

- **Praise** This works rather like a cuddle. A child loves to be praised. He's done something right. At last! Don't *you* like being told when you get something right?

- **Star chart**   Nice and straightforward for toddlers. Every time they sleep through the night or go straight to bed, they get a star. Pin the chart up on the kitchen wall or somewhere where they can see it. When adults visit, point it out and make your child feel good. When your child reaches a certain number of stars, you could reward him with a small present.

- **Reward box**   A variation on the above which might appeal to older children who think star charts are babyish. Leave a small shoebox under your child's bed. If he stays quiet through the night, you can slip a small 'reward' inside such as a crayon or colouring book. If he doesn't stay quiet through the night, it will remain disappointingly empty . . .

- **Special treat**   Verbal promises can mean more to older children from five upwards. Has your child been wanting to do something such as go to the playground? You could promise to take him there if he is quiet through the night for one week. Or you could buy him a new pair of pyjamas – another reason for going to bed fast.

No, it is *not* bribery even if it seems like it! Actually, it is a reward for good behaviour. And if it gets you there in the end, it might be worth it . . .

Make sure that your child always has to do a little more to achieve the same reward – otherwise no progress will be made. And remember, frequent small rewards are more effective than one large reward.

· *Positive discipline* ·

This could go hand-in-hand with giving your child a reward. Positive discipline is about putting things right that have been done wrong.

For example:

- If your child has gone up to bed half an hour later than you asked him to, he has to go to bed half an hour *earlier* the next night to make up for it. In other words, he has to pay himself back. Even toddlers can be taught to do this.

- If your child has disturbed you by calling out, he has to be particularly quiet on another occasion to 'make up' for his earlier noise.

- If your toddler has upset you by yelling or crying, he has to do something to make you feel better. This can be something as simple as drawing you a picture. But it will help him to see the point.

• CHAPTER EIGHT •
If all else fails

It doesn't work! You've tried to let your baby settle down in the middle of the night by himself. But he wouldn't. He just cried and cried.

Your toddler started wandering around the house at 2 a.m. and wouldn't go back to his own bed. When you took him into yours, he wriggled all night.

Your four-year-old woke up at 4 a.m. and wouldn't go back to sleep.

· *To smack or not to smack?* ·

It's tempting, isn't it? You've put your child to bed and he keeps coming back downstairs, turning up like a bad penny. You've run out of patience. And you feel like giving him a good smack. What's wrong with that?

Smacking won't make anyone happy. You want bedtime to be a pleasant time but if you smack your child, he won't be very happy. And he won't go to bed in the right frame of mind. He will also learn to associate bedtime with something unpleasant.

If you smack your child, the chances are that you'll feel guilty afterwards. Then you might well over-compensate by giving in: 'I shouldn't have smacked my child like that. Perhaps I should let him stay up later until we've made up.'

Emotions are catching. If you get angry, the chances are that your child will get angry too. You'll both lose control and then you'll be back to square one.

Stop yourself from getting cross by watching out for the following danger signs:

- You're saying things more than twice.
- You can feel yourself getting upset.
- You're saying things you don't really mean.

Then give yourself some breathing space by:

- Going to the lavatory for a few minutes.
- Washing your face.
- Going out of the room for a minute.

After that you have two options. You could:

1. Call it a day and give in. Let your child come downstairs or play. And put him to bed later.

   But if you do that, you'll be borrowing on that 'bank loan' we talked about. You'll be borrowing time and patience and will have to pay it back later. And in the long run, it will take longer for you to persuade your child that you are in charge.

Or you could:

2. Decide you're going to get cross but in a controlled way. Remember Chapter 3 about keeping your child in bed? You pretended you were an actor. You practised putting on a firm face which said, 'I mean what I'm saying'.

   Now you can put those acting lessons into practice. Look as though you mean what you're saying. '*Bed. Now.*' And remember, it's not negotiable.

· *John* ·

John's parents had always found him rather difficult to manage; he always seemed to be either crying or grizzling. When he was two he seemed to do the opposite of what they told him to do. The only way they could get John to do what they wanted was either to shout at him or smack him. The health visitor explained that it is normal for two-year-old children to do the opposite of what they are asked to do. This is called 'negativism'. Nevertheless, John continued to be miserable and difficult and his parents felt that they had to smack him or shout at him to get him to behave. John was particularly difficult in the evenings and this was when he got smacked the most. By the age of four, John had become really difficult to manage. He had been excluded from the day nursery because he kept hitting the other children. The situation became so serious that the parents asked their GP for specialist help. The GP explained to the parents that every time they smacked him it made him more likely to be aggressive and difficult in the future, even though it might be effective in the short term. It would be better to move to a system of reward that concentrated on teaching him to behave well. One of the problems with smacking is that it teaches children what they should not do but does not help them to know what they should do. John's father designed a chart to put on the kitchen wall. The chart was marked off in half-hour periods, from four o'clock to half-past six (bedtime). The parents cut out some small coloured stars and whenever John managed to go for half an hour without being disobedient, he was allowed to glue a star on his chart. John enjoyed this and became very proud of his chart, with all the colourful stars. Gradually, he became a much happier boy and his parents decided never to smack him again and tried not to shout at him.

· *What can I do?* ·

Take a break. If you don't feel able to start again, forget it – for a while. Go back to what you were doing before. But only do this for a short time until you can summon up enough energy to make a clean start. Then try again.

Start again. Take stock. Have another look at the questionnaire. Pinpoint areas which worked a bit, if not a hundred per cent, and try again. Maybe you need practice as much as your child. Perhaps you need convincing, too. So remember: practice makes perfect.

Can anyone else do a better job?   As a parent, it's tempting to think you're indispensable. No one else could calm your child down in the middle of the night. Or could they? If you have a grandparent, aunt, childminder, close friend, tell them about your sleeping problems. See if they could look after your baby or toddler or older child for a few nights – preferably in your own house where the child knows the layout. This may break the bad sleep habit.

Your substitute parent might have some bright ideas which you've been too tired or impatient to think of. It's amazing what a fresh eye can see!

Start a local self-help group.   Talk to other mothers. Ask your health visitor or doctor to put you in touch with other families whose children don't sleep.

Meet up for a chat. Maybe one of them has a good idea which might help you. Perhaps you have a suggestion which might help them.

Try reading this book together and following the guidelines. It's often easier if more than one of you are doing it at the same time. You could give each other emotional support and compare notes.

Give yourself an alternative helping hand.   Sometimes, alternative remedies can help sleeplessness. They might work for you in conjunction with some of this book's suggestions.

Try:

- *Lavender oil*. You can buy this from most health shops. Use it in very small quantities, according to the instructions. Try dabbing some on your child's skin – usually behind the ears – or on the bed sheets. But check with the bottle's instructions – or the shopkeeper – that the product is suitable for your child's age group as consistencies vary.

- *Homeopathy*. Visit your local health shop to see if they can suggest a homeopathic remedy for your child. The type will depend on your child's different needs. For more information, contact the Homeopathic Trust, Hahnemann House, 2 Powis Place, Great Ormond Street, London WC1N 3HT.

- *Massage* your baby or toddler with baby oil as part of his bedtime routine. This could make him feel more relaxed about going into his bed or cot.

- *Hang a prism* in your child's bedroom. This is said to concentrate good forces. It might be worth a try . . . but make sure that you hang it somewhere out of your child's reach. Amethyst crystal is also said to have a similar effect.

- *Give him some medicine.* Frankly, this really should be a last resort. Some doctors prescribe sleeping medicine for children or advise parents to buy certain cough medicines which contain a sedative. However, there is no real harm in using hypnotic drugs for a short time in an emergency.

· *Disadvantages of medicines* ·

- 'Sleepy medicines' often make children irritable the next day and may hype your child up.

- They disrupt your child's normal sleeping cycles. So it will be even more difficult to train him in a sleeping pattern which fits in with the house.

- You can't use them for ever. Children soon become tolerant of them and the effect wears off.

- When sleeping medicines are stopped, the child may find it more difficult to go to sleep than he did before taking the medicine.

- There is no sleep medicine that will keep any child asleep all night. The maximum time is four hours, otherwise the dose would make him dozy the next day.

CHAPTER NINE

Breaking the routine

Rigid bedtime patterns and routines are all very well, but sooner or later, something will happen which means you will have to break them.

Usually, these breaks are temporary, caused by minor illness or going on holiday. So always try to get back to normal as soon as you can before the new habits set in.

Other breaks to the routine, such as your child's daytime nap, may be more frequent.

· *Daytime napping* ·

Babies vary tremendously when it comes to napping. It can be very worrying when you listen to other mothers and wonder why your child isn't doing the same as their children. But babies are all different, just as you differ from other parents. It would be a boring world if we were all the same!

Some babies sleep deeply for three or even four hours at a time during the day. Others will wake far more often. But by the time they're between six months and a year, most will stay awake for most of the day and make do with one or two naps.

There's nothing wrong with that. It gives you time to get on with everything else you need to do. Until, that is, you want to start a more regular bedtime routine.

Did you know?

If children have a nap, they develop an increased attention span and are more relaxed and contented.

Nap chart showing the amount of time that babies/toddlers usually sleep during the day

Four months to 6 months:	Two to three times a day. Three to seven hours in total.
Six months to 12 months:	Once or twice a day. One to six hours in total.
Two years:	Once a day. One to three hours in total.
Four years:	Four times a week.

· *How to develop a good napping routine* · *without affecting the bedtime routine*

Try to encourage your older baby to have his first nap as soon as possible in the morning. You might be able to do this by taking him for a walk in his pram/pushchair or even a ride in the car so the motion helps him to sleep.

If he has a second nap, make sure it's either before or soon after lunch (wait until his food has gone down properly). Keep it short – try waking him after an hour or so. The longer the gap between the end of that final nap and bedtime, the more willing he'll be to go to bed. But make sure he is not getting overtired before bedtime.

On the other hand, if you put your baby to bed at night too early, he is more likely to wake up at 5 a.m. instead of a more civilised hour. You might find it works better to put him to bed latish in the evening – such as between 8 and 10 p.m. – so his sleeping hours coincide with yours.

At this stage, it's very much a matter of trial and error. If it doesn't work, try putting him down for his nap and final sleep at different times until you've both worked out a pattern.

Naps and older children

Between the ages of two and three, your toddler reaches a tricky stage. He might get crotchety and over-tired if he doesn't have a nap. But if he *does* have one – even a short one – he then won't feel like going to bed until much later in the evening. Some parents joke that a 20-minute nap is worth three hours of a proper sleep. In other words, if your child naps for 20 minutes, it costs you three hours of his sleep in the evening.

If you have older children whom you need to take or collect from somewhere in the afternoon, you'll probably find that your toddler drops off to sleep in the pram/car. He'll then wake full of life at 5 p.m. Bang goes your evening!

What to do:

- If your toddler gets very tired and upset because he doesn't have a daytime nap, his body is telling you he genuinely needs that rest – even if it doesn't fit in with your schedule. Try making that nap as early as possible (just as with younger children) by putting him down in his cot/bed.

- Bring your daytime routine forwards. If your toddler is over-tired without a daytime nap and is so exhausted that he falls asleep over tea, bring teatime forward to 4 p.m. and bed at 5 p.m.

- Re-think your day. Is it possible for someone else to bring home your older child in the afternoon? That way, your toddler won't fall asleep when you go to collect older siblings. If someone asks you out for tea and you know your younger children will fall asleep on the way back, see if you can meet earlier in the day instead. Perhaps your friend could come round to *you* instead.

This might sound as though you're fitting your own life around your child's. But it's only for a short time until his body clock learns to manage without a daytime sleep.

Summer/winter

Isn't it wonderful? Just as you've got your child into a routine, the clocks change. Suddenly, we're an hour later or an hour earlier than we were yesterday. It's hard enough for some adults to cope with. So think what it's like for your child . . .

What to do:

- Nothing for older babies and younger toddlers. Stick to your usual routine at the (new) time by the clock on their bedroom wall. There's no need for them to realise that anything is different. Most children – and adults – adapt quickly to changing bedtime by one hour.

- Use that clock for older and more street-wise toddlers and children. When they say, 'Why do I have to go to bed? It's still light outside', point to the clock. You could try explaining the time change in simple terms. For example, 'Now it's summer, it's lighter, but it's still time to go to bed. Look at the clock – you always go to bed at 7 p.m.'

- Buy heavier curtains to shut out the light. A cheaper option is a pair of curtain liners – available from most curtain shops – which you hang between the curtain and the window to make your child's bedroom darker.

Babysitters

At last! You're going out for the evening. You haven't had a night off for months. But will your babysitter be able to get your child to bed happily?

Going out for the evening is a double-edged sword, isn't it? You want to get out but you don't. Supposing your child can't go to sleep without you? Will a babysitter destroy the routine which you have so carefully built up?

Relax. One night isn't going to spoil everything. But you *can* make things as smooth as possible.

- Make sure your babysitter is mature, reliable, experienced and has references (always check them). Write down your contact number on the kitchen noticeboard or the phone book: a flimsy scrap of paper might get lost. Also, leave one other emergency number in case she or he can't reach you.

- Introduce your sitter to your children at least once – and preferably more often – before the evening. Even if your baby is too young to recognise her, it will give your sitter a chance to get familiar with your family. Watch how your sitter holds/plays with/talks to your child. If she's more interested in how the television works or her rates of pay, think again.

- Explain your child's bedtime routine to your sitter. Also write it down clearly (e.g., 6.00 Bath. 6.15 Story. 6.30 Lights out). Give her the 'magic' bedtime phrase such as 'Goodnight. Sleep Tight' which will make your child feel reassured. Leave out comforters and explain where drinks are, etc.

- Ask your sitter to stick to the routine as closely as possible. But if your child seems very upset without you, she can adapt it accordingly. For example, she might need to stay by your child's bed instead of saying goodnight and going out as you have learned to do.

- Try to get babies and younger toddlers to sleep before you go out. Explain to older toddlers and children that your sitter will be there if they wake up. It can be terrifying for a child to wake up and find that someone else is there if you haven't warned them in advance.

- Don't stay out too long when using a sitter for the first time.

- If you're leaving your children with a friend still explain the routine. Tell your friend how important it is to you to keep this pattern going.

But also remember that it might be more difficult for a friend to stick to this especially if she has children of her own and is doing you a favour in having yours.

If she's only looking after your children for one evening, this doesn't matter so much. As we've said, routines can sometimes be broken. The important point is to make sure they are not broken for too long.

· *George* ·

George's parents used to enjoy going out and seeing friends in the evenings before he was born. After his birth, as they could not afford a regular babysitter, they decided to take George with them when they went out. They were surprised at how easy it was to put George into the carrycot and take him anywhere at night. He would settle surprisingly well ... until he was about seven months old. It then became progressively difficult to get him settled; he didn't take kindly to strangers or to unfamiliar places. When they checked with their health visitor they discovered that this was not at all surprising because it is at around the age of six to eight months that children begin to recognise the outside world and distinguish between what is familiar and what is strange. It is at this point that they develop 'stranger anxiety'. In most cases this settles down between the ages of three and four and it is again possible to take children with you for an evening out and, provided they are given clear instructions about what they can and can't do and they have a comfortable bed to go to sleep in, there are usually no problems.

· *Going on holiday* ·

Why is it that you've been looking forward to your holiday for so long but are now full of doubts? Will your child be able to sleep on the plane or will he run around, annoying everyone? Will you be able to keep him awake on the car journey so he goes down to bed at the normal time when you reach your destination? Should you dose with sleeping medicine so he nods off at the right time? Will the bed/cot be safe at your holiday hotel/cottage/apartment?

Sleeping during the journey

Sometimes it helps if your baby/toddler/older child sleeps on the way. It might disrupt his evening bedtime routine but it's only for one night. If you've already established a good pattern, this is unlikely to scupper it!

On the other hand, 'helping' him to sleep with medication isn't always a good idea (see Chapter 8: If all else fails). Sleeping medicines can sometimes work the other way and make your child over-active or grumpy when he wakes up. If you really want to give him something, always check with your GP first, and try out the medicine on your child at home before a journey to see what the effect is.

Pack a travel bag with sleep in mind

Make sure you have all the necessary sleeping comforts (comforter, bedtime storybook, pillow, etc.) for your child's routine. Then, when you reach your destination, you have everything to hand instead of having to search through bulging suitcases on the hotel floor or in the car boot!

TIP: If you want to keep your older toddler/child awake during the journey, pack a surprise bag of goodies to stop him falling asleep. For example, you could put in a colouring book, crayons, magic slate for drawing, simple puzzle, etc.

The holiday bedroom

If you're booking through a travel agency, ask someone to check that the cot/bed conforms to British Standards or carries the CE European safety mark.

When you get there, check the cot carefully for loose bolts or anything which might be swallowed by young children.

- Does the mattress fit snugly or could your child's face get trapped between the mattress and frame?

- Are the bars on the cot wide enough for your child to get stuck in between? Is the cot on castors? If so, it could move when you don't want it to.

- Is the bedroom safe, generally? Can your child fall out of the window or balcony? Are there different floor levels which might trip him up?

Sometimes you can improvise by:

- Blocking the cot between two single beds so it doesn't move.

- Putting furniture obstacles in place so your child can't get onto the balcony.

If you're worried, see your holiday representative/hotel manager, etc.

TIP: To reassure your child, take his duvet cover to make the cot/bed feel more like his own at home.

TIP: Take your mobile baby monitor with you, providing it works on batteries or you have an adapter. One mother always finds out, before she books a holiday, what the distance is from the hotel dining room to the child's bedroom to check it's within range of the baby monitor. That way, she can enjoy an evening meal and know she can hear her child if something goes wrong.

Have fun

Holidays are for fun, so enjoy your break. At the same time, try to stick to your child's routine without being a stick-in-the-mud. If you want to go out to eat in the evening but your child is usually asleep by 8 p.m., try eating earlier.

If he normally has an afternoon nap but you want to go out, take the pushchair/stroller/pram so he can still have his sleep.

Back to normal

When you come back from holiday, get back into your bedtime routine as soon as possible. Hopefully, you won't have deviated from it too much anyway . . .

· *School holidays* ·

If you have older children at school, it's tempting to let them sleep in later than usual during the holidays. The problem is that you might do the same and so will your younger ones – especially if you've let bedtime become later as there isn't any school the next day.

By the time the new term arrives – and you need to get everyone to bed on time – your routine might have fallen by the wayside! So try:

- Sticking more closely to what you usually do but allowing older children more lee-way. For example, they could stay up (or lie in) half an hour longer than usual. But don't let it become much longer or it will be more difficult to get back to the old sleep cycle. Try keeping to your usual boundaries for younger children.

- A week before term starts, go back to the old routine. If it doesn't work, you've got time to sort it out before the term actually begins!

CHAPTER TEN

Older children

When your children are small, you assume that life will get easier when they reach the age of five. After all, they'll be able to feed themselves, take themselves to the lavatory, go to school and sleep through the night. Won't they?

Perhaps it's just as well that we don't find out the real answer until they get to that age. Otherwise, we might not have the strength to go on! But the truth is that children can continue to have sleeping problems right up to teenage years and into adulthood. Even then, you still won't get any sleep because you'll be wondering what they're up to . . . !

· *'I don't want to go to bed'* ·

This is the stage when television/video becomes a real temptation. 'All my friends watch it until 9 p.m. so why can't I?'

What to do:
Stand by your own beliefs. Decide what you feel is the right bedtime and stick to it. Remember the routine you followed when your child was a toddler. Well, devise another which is suitable for your child's age, and don't let it out of your sight. If bathtime is at 7.30 and bed at 8 p.m., that stands even if he does want to watch something at 8.30 p.m.

Easier said than done?

Make a joke out of it. Point out adults of your acquaintance who look tired or have heavy eye bags. Ask your child if he wants to look like that. Point out that he needs to sleep in order to grow.

· *'I can't sleep'* ·

It's not a nice feeling, lying in your bed unable to sleep. You know you ought to but you simply can't. As an adult, you probably recognise that feeling. But it's scary for an older child.

What to do:

- Tell him, 'That's fine. You don't need to fall asleep; just rest'.

- Don't encourage him to read or do something active. That's not resting. He's already had time to read a book before proper bedtime. Although there is nothing wrong with reading at night, it is not possible to read and go to sleep at the same time. Also, the reading could soon become part of the sleep habit and will then persist – possibly for ever. Instead, encourage him to read at another time.

- Encourage your child to think back through his day, backwards. This gets progressively more difficult – the morning will seem a long time away. But that's good because the effort in remembering will make him feel sleepier.

- Joke about it. Tell him to try to stay awake if he can't sleep.

- Is your child physically comfortable? Is he warm enough? Is his bed still suitable? If your older child is still sleeping in the bed he had as a five- or six-year-old, it might be too narrow or short. Perhaps the mattress has become lumpy. Maybe he needs a firmer one now to cope with his increased body weight.

· *How much sleep does your older* · *child need?*

Older children tend to go through phases of sleeping for longer periods than when they were younger. They might well sleep for more than 12 hours.

On the other hand, older children sometimes get a buzz out of not sleeping because of the strange 'out of body' experiences it can cause.

TIP: If you've got younger children who are already in bed, use this 'spare' time as a special time to talk to your older children before they turn out the lights.

Older children sometimes complain about being 'neglected' because Mum is paying more attention to younger siblings – especially if they're playing up.

Now the little ones are in bed, there's time to give that extra one-to-one attention – even a few minutes is enough. Have a chat about the day over a cup of hot chocolate. Or dust down your old childhood books and read to your older children. Even though they can read to themselves, they'll probably enjoy someone else reading to them, too. It's part of a soothing wind-down bedtime routine. You'll be surprised at how much you can enjoy this special time, too. It will also bring you closer to your children during those awkward adolescent years.

However, it is best to keep this special time quite short – about five to 10 minutes – so that it ends while your child is still enjoying it and has not become bored.

TIP: Don't allow your child to have a television in his bedroom because:

- You can't be sure what your child is watching.

- Bedrooms are designed for sleep.

- If you allow your child to go to sleep watching television, it becomes a habit. He might also go to sleep without turning it off. This might be dangerous.

'I can't get my older child up in the morning'

- Give him plenty of warning.
- Draw the curtains or put on the light at least 10 minutes before he needs to get up.
- Point out that if he went to bed earlier, he'd wake up on time.
- Make sure he still has a clock or a watch in his room. Then make him responsible for his own time-keeping. If he's late for school, he will be the one to get a detention, not you . . .

· *Rules are made to be broken* ·

Every now and then, it's fun to do something you shouldn't.

There's no harm in your older child chatting for half the night to a friend who is staying overnight. It's a one-off, so don't be too hard. It's fun, after all.

The same goes for late nights. If your child goes out on a Saturday night, fine – providing you're happy with the circumstances.

But he'll still need an early night during the week when there's school next day. And you still need to be firm in telling him so – just as you did when he was little, and even if he's now as tall as you!

After all, you're still feeding him and providing a roof over his head, aren't you? And while he's in your house, he still has to follow your rules. Don't be scared of telling him – but make it fun, too. Promise him that when *he* has a house of his own and you come to stay, you'll follow *his* house rules!

CHAPTER ELEVEN

Time for you

You might think that your child's sleep is only important for him. After all, it will help him to grow – both physically and mentally – because it's teaching him self-dependence.

But a good sleeping pattern for children is also vital for you in lots of different ways.

We've already talked about how important it is to have an evening on your own. This isn't being selfish. It's a basic need – just as you need food and drink.

Being a parent can be rather like working on a pleasurable assembly line: you love the things you're making (in other words, your children). You want to be doing the job, e.g., being with them. But you have to put components (clothes/food/drink/sleep) on them all day long. You have to do the same jobs, day in and day out.

Like every manual worker, you need a coffee break. In other words, a time to re-charge your batteries. But, unlike most factory workers, you haven't got a union to make sure you get these rights. Instead you have to battle for them yourself.

If you can succeed in getting your children into a bedtime routine, you'll be able to achieve that goal of time for yourself. When things are going wrong and you feel like giving up and doing what your children want instead of what you want, remember that goal.

· You and your partner ·

You don't need time just for yourself. You also need time for your partner – or, if you don't have one, time to talk to other people and maybe go out.

Health visitors occasionally joke that children are one of

the best contraceptives available. Sadly, that's true especially if your children regularly hop into bed with you during the night – or you put them into your bed in the first place to get them to sleep.

Some parents carry on anyway. But there will come a stage when your child is aware of what is going on. Even if you don't mind, it could well lead to embarrassing situations – especially when your little one goes to school and happens to tell the teacher! In any case, it is a form of abuse to expose children to adult sexuality: it only confuses them and encourages them to experiment themselves.

Only you can decide what bedtime patterns are right for you. But it's worth remembering all the pros and cons:

'We don't see things the same way'

When you first met your partner, you probably talked about what kind of music you liked; what books you liked to read; where you came from; how many brothers and sisters you had, etc. But you probably didn't ask each other about child-rearing and what you did or didn't believe in!

It's not surprising then that when you have a child, you may disagree about how you should bring that child up. If he doesn't want to eat his supper, one of you might think he should be made to, and the other might think he should be let off.

The same goes for sleeping. Maybe you think your wandering toddler should be firmly escorted back to bed, but your partner thinks he should be allowed to come into your bed so you can have some rest.

Try to:

- Talk about it.
- See each other's point of view.
- Try each other's methods out and see what works.
- Remember that you'll still need each other when your baby grows up and no longer needs you.

- Recall what brought you together in the first place and try to re-kindle that interest.

- Make a special effort when you *are* finally alone. Cook a candle-lit dinner or book a babysitter.

· *How to wean yourself from your* · *child at night*

That's right: it's not always the child who has to be weaned. Often a parent – who's especially close to a child – has to learn to let go at night. He or she has to learn that a child can sleep safely on his own.

Maybe your child is the youngest and you have an understandable need to 'baby' him more or perhaps he's a very much wanted child after a miscarriage or several years of trying.

So it's not surprising that you find it difficult to 'let go' at night. If he cries, your immediate reaction is to rush in. When he's asleep, you might constantly be checking him.

What to do:

- Accept that your feelings are natural.

- Make sure your child is well and that his room is safe.

- Allow yourself to check him at limited times, e.g., once during the evening and maybe once during the night. Reduce this just as you reduced the amount of time you spent in his bedroom when he wanted you to stay.

- Tell yourself that you're helping him by encouraging him to establish a good sleeping routine. Just as you're helping him when you prepare a healthy meal or walk him down the street safely, taking care not to go near the traffic.

· *Your own sleeping patterns as a child* ·

We're often told that we carry our childhood experiences around with us like baggage. And it can be true.

What was your own experience of sleeping when you were a child? If you were scared of the dark, the chances are that you might pass on these fears to a child. So, stop yourself before it's too late. Remind yourself that being scared of the dark didn't help you. So don't pass on the same legacy to your own children who in turn might then pass it on to their children.

Were you forced to go to bed early when all your friends were allowed to watch television or listen to the radio? Perhaps that's now making you move in the opposite direction, away from a routine. That's fine if it's what you want. But think again. Did a routine do you any harm? Could you not compromise and allow your child some freedom in the evening while keeping him to the rules which you want him to follow?

Did you have to share a room with a brother or sister? If so, you might have hated it. Perhaps you wanted your own space. So now you've put your children in different rooms. Do they want to be apart? Might they actually enjoy each other's company and feel comforted by it? Or would they chat too much and disrupt each other's routine? You can only tell by trying out the different alternatives and seeing what works for you.

· *Your health and happiness* ·

These can deeply affect how well your child sleeps. Is it possible that you might be depressed? If so, this might be rubbing off on your children who might then find it hard to go to sleep. It might also stop you from thinking rationally and calmly when you're trying to get them into a routine.

Don't be scared of going to see the doctor. Depression nowadays is not a stigma. Many new parents – and old ones – feel low or clinically depressed. But it is possible to do something about it. Your GP will show you how. And if he or she isn't sympathetic, perhaps you should find one who *is*.

• CONCLUSION •
My child still isn't sleeping!

If you've read this book and you still have a problem, there's no need to throw it across the room in a rage! Instead, remind yourself that:

- Sleeplessness in children is a very common problem.
- Bringing up children is hard work but very rewarding.
- You can always try again. Put away the book for a few weeks and then read it once more. You might feel able to tackle issues you couldn't tackle when you first tried.
- Remember that sleep will come in the end. What counts is that you and your child have peaceful and restful nights.
- It is worth putting a lot of effort into creating a good sleep routine. It will help your child mature and will improve many other aspects of family life.
- If you are finding it difficult, don't hesitate to ask for help – you are not alone.

Making an investment

Having a child is like putting your savings into an account. It's making an investment for the future. You are putting a lot of your own time, effort and love into your child. And one day, all that hard work will pay off. It may take years – just like it takes years for interest on a savings account to build up – but you will get it in the end!

Like a savings account, your investment will go up and down. **But if you hold on, you will get there in the end**.

Sometimes, you'll find yourself taking out some of your investment. You could see this as deviating from the sleeping routine every now and then, but that's alright. You can enjoy breaking the rules occasionally.

Then you can go back to basics. Or read the book again! Goodnight . . .

Index

OTHER PARENTING TITLES PUBLISHED BY VERMILION

The Great Ormond Street New Baby and Child Care Book
by Tessa Hamilton and Maire Messenger
ISBN 0 09 181712 9

Aromatherapy and Massage for Mother and Baby
by Allison England
ISBN 0 09 182275 0

Toddler Taming
by Dr Christopher Green
ISBN 0 09 177258 3

Understanding ADHD
by Dr Christopher Green
ISBN 0 09 181700 5

Natural Babycare
by Julia Goodwin
ISBN 0 09 186983 8

Baby Love
by Robin Barker
ISBN 0 09 182425 7

The Guide to Your Child's Symptoms
edited by Dr David Haslam
ISBN 0 09 181603 3

**To order a copy, simply phone our credit card hotline
on 01206 255800**